HINTERLAND

Hinterland offers an a[...]
question 'what is creati[...]
by showcasing the best [...]
the fields of memoir, essay, travel and
food writing, reportage, psychoscape,
biography, flash non-fiction and more.

Our pages bring together work by
established, award-winning authors
alongside new writers, many of whom
we are thrilled to publish for the first time
and whose work, we promise, will merit
your full attention.

Often, the pieces you'll find in Hinterland
will straddle the boundaries between
strands and be difficult to classify:
we see this as a strength. Hinterland
intends to challenge, move, entertain
and, above all, be a fantastic read.

WELCOME TO ISSUE 8

Advocates for Hinterland:
Nathan Hamilton, Kathryn Hughes,
Helen Smith, Rebecca Stott, Ian Thomson

Editorial Team
Editors-In-Chief – Freya Dean & Andrew Kenrick
Art Direction & Design – Tom Hutchings
Marketing Manager – Kate Simpson
Business Support – Ben Watkins
Proofreaders – Susan K. Burton, Margaret Hedderman, Yin F. Lim,
                    Stephen Massil, Aaron O'Farrell, Florence Pearce-
                    Higginson, Claire Reiderman and Isabel Williams

Submissions
Hinterland is committed to paying writers and artists for all work we publish.
Please send us your work via Submittable:
hinterlandnonfiction.submittable.com
We accept submissions year-round and endeavour to reply within 4 months.
We regret we are unable to provide feedback.
There is a small fee of £3 per submission.

Subscriptions
An annual subscription to Hinterland (four issues, print and digital)
costs £40 U.K., £44 Europe, £54 Rest-of-world.
Digital subscription only, £20.
Please visit our website for full details.

Distribution
Hinterland is distributed worldwide by NBN International.
For all trade orders contact +44 (0) 1752 202301
orders@nbninternational.com

Advertising
Please see our website for current rates, or to discuss sponsorship please
contact us at hinterlandnonfiction@gmail.com

Acknowledgments
The Editors gratefully acknowledge financial contributions from
the UEA Publishing Project.

Find Hinterland online at
www.hinterlandnonfiction.com
or contact us: hinterlandnonfiction@gmail.com

ISBN: 978-1-913861-14-8
ISSN (Print): 2632-136X
ISSN (Online): 2632-1378

HINTERLAND

THE BEST NEW CREATIVE NON-FICTION

Issue 8
2021

Issue 8

Contributors

Amy Cotler (*Sally's Cake*) is a chef and writer. Her short pieces have appeared in various publications, including right here in *Hinterland*, as well as *Guesthouse*, *The Rambling Epicure* and *Bright Flash*. Before turning to creative writing, Cotler worked as a food writer, cooking teacher and cookbook author. She was a leader of the farm-to-table movement in the US, and food forum host for *The New York Times*. Currently, she lives in Mexico with her husband, an artist, and their dog, Remy. Visit her at amycotler.com

Sally Gander (*The Pen: A Collection*) writes fiction and creative nonfiction. Her work has appeared in *Litro*, *Backlash Press*, *Porridge*, *The Lincoln Review*, *The Blue Nib* and *Elsewhere*. For many years she taught Creative Writing at Bath Spa University, and now teaches students from across the world at Advanced Studies in England. You can read her blog and more of her published work at sallymgander.blog

Connor Harrison (*11th March, Montmartre*) is a writer based in the West Midlands. His work has appeared at *Lit Hub*, *New Critique*, *Longleaf Review* and *Review31*, among others.

Andrew Kenrick (*On Meat*) is a founding editor of this magazine.

Edward Little (*A Mind Full of Sake*) is a writer from the Wirral who studied for an MA in Creative Writing at Chester. He has been published in a variety of online and print magazines, including *Storgy*, *Cagibi*, *Pandora's Box*, and others. Spending a lot of time at open-mic events, he turns stories like this one into performances, hoping to soon have a collection that attracts readers as well as a live audience. This one is dedicated to drunk encounters.

Maya Osman-Krinsky (*Pork Belly Prayer*; they/them) is a native New Yorker who writes about the relationships between language, food, and violence. Maya graduated with a BA in Linguistics from the University of Chicago in 2021 and is now pursuing a Masters in Public Health at Columbia University. Maya is a Pushcart nominee, was named runner-up in the 2020 Kurt Brown Prize for Creative Nonfiction, and participated in the 2021 Tin House Summer Workshop. Their writing can be found in *Hinterland*, *Stone of Madness*, *Brevity*, *Bite Magazine*, and *Food Tank*. Keep up with Maya on Twitter at @mokwrites

Pragya Agarwal (*The Slow Dance*) is a behavioural and data scientist. She has a PhD from Nottingham University and is a Visiting Professor of Inequities and Social Inclusion at Loughborough University. Pragya is the author of *Sway: Unravelling Unconscious Bias* and *Wish We Knew What to Say: Talking with Children about Race*. She has also written for The *Guardian, Prospect, New Scientist, Literary Hub, AEON, Scientific American* and the *Wellcome Collection,* amongst others. Her most recent book *(M)otherhood: On the choices of being a woman* is out now. She came to the UK almost 20 years ago and now lives in the north-west next to the sea. Pragya loves to read about food, think about food, dream about food. She can be found on Twitter @drpragyaagarwal and at drpragyaagarwal.com.

Noah Birksted-Breen (*Snow*) translated and directed contemporary Russian plays for staging in the UK for his ensemble Sputnik Theatre Company (www.sputniktheatre.co.uk) for over fifteen years. In 2017, he completed a PhD at Queen Mary University of London, and subsequently worked for three years as a researcher of contemporary Russian culture for Creative Multilingualism at the University of Oxford. Noah is a Researcher in Oxford's School of Geography and the Environment and is currently completing an MA in Creative Writing at Birkbeck. In 2019 he was the 'Hackney Winner' of Spread the Word's *City of Stories* competition. In 2021, 'Beef' was published in *The Real Story,* and three eco-poems appeared in *The Mechanics' Institute Review.*

Kimmo Rosenthal (*The Little Patch of Yellow Wall*) has turned from a career in mathematics and teaching to writing. His most recent work has appeared in *Indefinite Space*, *The Decadent Review*, *The Fib Review*, *After the Art*, *Hinterland*, *The Dillydoun Review*, and is forthcoming in *BigCityLit*. He also has a Pushcart Prize nomination and is a non-fiction Staff Reader for *Ploughshares*.

Kate Young (*The Promise of a Dinner Party*) is an award-winning food writer, cook and bookworm. Her Little Library Cookbooks (*The Little Library Cookbook*, *The Little Library Year*, and *The Little Library Christmas*) feature food inspired by famous, beloved and occasionally obscure works of literature. She has written about food, books, sexuality, and dungarees for various publications, including *The Guardian*, *Prospect Magazine*, *Slightly Foxed*, *Stylist*, *Delicious*, and *Sainsbury's Magazine*. After a sunny Australian childhood spent indoors reading books, she moved to London, which suited her much better. She is now based in the English countryside. You can follow her on Twitter and Instagram (@bakingfiction).

Sarah Young (*Writing My Mother*) lives in Wellington, New Zealand. She completed a Master of Arts in Creative Writing (Prose) at the University of East Anglia in 2014, where she was the UEA Booker scholarship recipient. Her non-fiction work has been published in *Strong Words 2*. She has been shortlisted for the Sozopol Fiction Seminar Fellowship in Bulgaria and the Newsroom Surrey Hotel Writers Residency and her fiction was long-listed for the Bath Short Story award and the BBC National Short Story award in the UK. She formerly worked as a journalist in Dubai, Indonesia, and New Zealand.

Hester van Hensbergen (*Eating Tongues of Songbirds*) is an intellectual historian and food writer with an interest in the relationship between food, politics, and environment. Her writing has appeared in *Vittles*, *Eater*, and *Still Point Journal*.

Tom Hutchings (*Picnic Blanket*) is our in-house graphic designer and cover artist. He's a freelance graphic designer specialising in print design, and can eat his own body weight in crisps given the opportunity. Have a look at his work on thorngraphicdesign.com

Sue Hann (*Recipes from my Father*) is a writer based in London. She is a Spread the Word London Writers Awards recipient 2019-20. Her work was long-listed for the Spread the Word Life Writing Prize 2020. She won the Diana Woods Memorial Award in 2020. Her flash fiction came Highly Commended National Flash Fiction Day 2019 Micro Competition. Her work has been published in journals such as *Popshot Quarterly, Longleaf Review, Multiplicity Magazine, Lunchticket, One Hand Clapping, Lunate Fiction, Ellipsis Zine, Fewer than 500, Funny Pearls* and *Litro Online,* as well as various flash fiction anthologies. You can find her on Twitter @SYwrites.

Anna Jones (*In Conversation with...*) is an award-winning cook, writer, the voice of modern vegetarian cooking and the author of the bestselling *A Modern Way to Eat, A Modern Way to Cook, The Modern Cook's Year,* and most recently, *One.* She lives, writes and cooks in Hackney, East London.

Editorial

The theme of food writing around which many (though not all) pieces in this issue coalesce, was driven by a number of outstanding submissions that used food as an entry point into other subjects. Often, as in the case of Amy Cotler, Sue Hann and Pragya Agarwal, it is a route into unpicking relationships with family or friends; or as in the pieces by Edward Little, Andrew Kenrick and Hester van Hensbergen, it is a way of understanding ourselves — the scraps of illumination that follow from being immersed in other places and other times, with distinct cultures and cuisines.

Kate Young, of *The Little Library Cafe*, explores the plain joy of sharing food in 'The Promise of a Dinner Party', while Anna Jones, whose entire catalogue of books are enjoyed and revered by so many, is our interview subject. Elsewhere in these pages is a

Freya Dean is of Dutch-British descent. She graduated from UEA's Creative Writing MA where she received the Lorna Sage award and, the same year, was an Elizabeth Kostova Foundation Finalist. Recent work features in *The Real Story*, *Visual Verse* and UEA's Anthology series.

devastating and beautifully told piece, 'Writing My Mother', by Sarah Young; 'Snow' by Noah Birksted-Breen, offers a piece of memoir set in St. Petersburg that would have pleased Tolstoy with its cast of characters. There is a hybrid essay 'Pen' by Sally Gander; and a gem of a piece of ekphrasis 'The Little Patch of Yellow Wall' by Kimmo Rosenthal.

Our next issue will herald a handful of changes at Hinterland. Yin F. Lim joins our team as co-editor, allowing Freya to take a year-long sabbatical (in which to complete a PGCE). We also say a huge thank you and farewell to Kate Simpson, who has provided her expert and generous marketing support over the last six months. Very happily, Hinterland continues to grow – thank you for reading and being a part of that.

Freya & Andrew

Andrew Kenrick has worked as an archaeologist and an archivist, a writer and an editor. He is currently studying for a PhD at the University of East Anglia, where he also teaches English Literature and Publishing.

Eating Tongues of Songbirds

by Hester van Hensbergen

The unfamiliar soup is a thin, brown, algae-coloured broth with sunken orzo at its base, served in a tin bowl. The first spoon brings an intense and surprisingly fulsome hit of cardamom. Then, in a slower release, come the cinnamon and nutmeg. The sweet fat of the chicken stock catches the whole mouthful and softens it. It also – almost imperceptibly – thickens the soup so that, after each scoop of the spoon agitates the orzo upwards, they sink back slowly, half-suspended, through the liquid to the bottom of the basin. Orzo pasta is usually compared to rice, but its Spanish name — piñones, pine nuts — offers a better visual cue. The Arabic word is more lyrical: lisaan al-3usfur, meaning 'the tongues of songbirds'.

I ate this soup once, at the beginning of a meal in a backstreet restaurant in Bab Al-Louq in central Cairo in the spring of 2013. The memory of the dishes that followed swims more mistily around that first cosmic liquid. I was eighteen and in the city for the second time; there to study Arabic, and staying with a journalist friend. We ate well, I remember. And we ate what we were given. Everything clattered to the table in metallic spheres: an entire chicken, hummus slicked with oil, flatbread piled like pillows, tomatoes and onions curing in vinaigrette, and rice. The rice was plain, rather than koshary — the carbalicious national dish of rice, pasta, lentils, caramelised onions, and spicy tomato sauce, which is its own meal. It would be Egypt's answer to the chip butty, if they didn't have that too – it's called a sandwich batata.

The restaurant was as spare as possible. The narrow kitchen opened directly onto the street, obstructed at the entrance by a makeshift wooden counter on wheels, where dishes were waiting. Three or four small tables in the low-lit alley served as the dining room. This was khamseen season, when desert sand blows frequently over the city and through doors, balconies, and windows, into every nook. It had already destroyed my friend's laptop. Maintaining the row of clean outdoor tables was itself a sign of attentiveness. The restaurant was a family operation: she cooked and he served, working seamlessly. Then there was the telephone, with their daughter on the other end of the line, keen to practise her English, and my friend was beckoned over to speak with her. The phone was curiously large, straight from the 1980s, and its fluorescent orange keys illuminated his face. That is the only photographic evidence I have of the meal: a grainy picture of my companion on the call, standing in their blue and white tiled kitchen. Our host beams warmly beside him.

The dinner was good, particularly in contrast to what we had eaten on previous evenings. A takeaway order for quail had yielded something that looked more like a small rodent; what was suggested by scale and shape was confirmed by the discovery of an incongruous tail. Anatomy doesn't lie. There had been a dystopian dinner in the Grand Nile Tower Hotel's Revolving Restaurant, where the khamseen sands obscured the promised panoramic views of the city. The only illumination came from flickering constellations studded into the ceiling, and an ineffectual table lamp. Through the gloom, I struggled to identify the overcooked edibles our indifferent waiter served – soggy vegetable matter, tough red meat. Intimacy was clearly the intended effect, but there was an uncomfortable edge: the hotel restaurant, like all others at that time, was all but deserted. Romance gave way to seediness in the artificial starlight.

As we sat over our bowls of fatty cardamom liquor, unwelcome thoughts of the jaded operation at the Revolving Restaurant seeped away. The soup, with its lilting orzo and completely new flavours, seemed to invite pause. I appreciated the invitation. Beyond the inevitable bustle of a city of more than nine million, we were only a few streets away from Tahrir Square. It felt as if each night brought the sounds of tear gas explosions, and each day brought new laws and more arrests. I was learning politics far more quickly than the pitiful progress I displayed at the language school.

Grim retrospect has cast the memory of that soup into even firmer suspense; the liquid is now a resin catching the falling birds' tongues in mid-flow along their descent. Things were happening then, of course. Each morning, on the balcony of my friend's apartment, I drank cardamom coffee and chewed over slightly gristly bread (the government-subsidised flatbread eaten by everyone, good despite the gristle, and central to the protests that had precipitated the revolution). Looking onto the Coptic Church opposite, I watched sand billow over rooftops and drank until my teeth and tongue clogged with sweet grains. In the week after I left Cairo, Coptic Christians would be killed in sectarian violence. At the funerals, more would die in clashes while police looked on. That violent spring transitioned to the deadliest summer.

I have since felt guilty and uncomfortable that I was in Cairo that spring at all, eating chicken soup and a rodent, learning pedestrian phrases, admiring the political minds of others, amused in taxis by the absurd traffic, and later geographically immune to what followed.

Between then and there, and here and now, there is so much distance. The deaths come from a different, though no less political, violence. The spaces of geographic immunity are like shifting tectonic plates, now sliding, then rapidly colliding.

For a while, there were songbirds and silence, not car horns and flares.

In the viscous time of lockdown, with nowhere to travel but backwards, I kept returning to that pensive dish, perched on its rickety table. I wondered how it has shaped my desires. That soup was, and is, so singular. But it taught me the high importance of stock and changed the palette of my young taste buds. It opened them up to the possibility of a broth as a silken fatty platform for other aromas. I like stock that way now, steeped with cardamom or cinnamon, but also (especially for fish) saffron, dry sherry, and star anise. The broth was an exposure, as tasting a wholly new food can be, shocking you into new wants and sensibilities. It settles as a powerful sensory kernel deep inside, to be thrown into the present unexpectedly. And so I find myself staring back into that tender liquid again. I pause to see the golden tongues oscillate downwards and watch anxiously for how they will eventually settle. **H**

LONDON LIT LAB

Online courses in 2021–22, for beginner to advanced writers:
- Flash Fiction: The Tiniest of Stories
- How to Write a Memoir Proposal
- Enchantment in Fiction
- Creative Nonfiction: Compelling Memoir
- Saltwater Folk Tales
- and many more!

Or join a **live online masterclass**, including:
- Nature writing with Stephen Moss
- Therapeutic writing workshop with Katie Watson
- How to pitch your writing with Ben Dunn

Join our community and nurture your talent in a supportive environment with like-minded people, where writers teach writers.

'Lily and Zoe offer teaching and coaching at the highest level. Their workshops have a reputation for encouraging excellence and creativity in a supportive environment. I am always recommending them.'
Julia Bell, Course Convenor, MA Creative Writing, Birkbeck.

www.londonlitlab.co.uk

Sally's Cake

by Amy Cotler

It isn't just about her eggs or even her cake. Sally comes back to me in other ways. When the paper's open to a Sudoku puzzle she would have clobbered in minutes. Or when the spine of *Middlemarch* is sticking out from its shelf, beckoning me back – *Read it again*, she would say.

Mostly Sally's my food whisperer, there in the aroma of borscht bubbling in my kitchen or in the first bite of, yes, a freshly baked cake. Or even when I spot one of those especially silly cakes, shaped like a bird or a baseball or a Teddy bear, sitting proudly in a bakery shop window.

Sally's Giant Green Boat Cake was a lark, but a paid lark, a job I'd handed over because I was never a passionate cake maker. Hers had a fish and nautical rope, all in icing, of course. Made for a series of recipe cards, photographed with assembly instructions, they were mailed to subscribers more interested in themes and shapes than flavor. Neither of us wanted to eat the thing. And so Sally, who had a frugal streak but a generous heart, stuck the cake in the tree outside her kitchen window for the birds.

Why do I daydream about a cake for the birds when Sally's real birthday cakes were glorious explorations of what flour, butter and farm fresh eggs could achieve together? Light and fluffy layered cakes with toasted coconut shavings. Sweet, lemony loaves, with a remote bitterness of zest. Who else could take on the challenge to bake mine with as much hazelnut flavor as possible, and to come up with a smooth kind of praline spread between each layer to do the trick. And who would encase my celebration cake with a chocolate-hazelnut buttercream of the gods.

Yes, I tend to look back in glory, even going so far as to imagine cakes unmade. So, for balance, I have to admit that your endless talking (and lack of listening) sometimes drove me insane. But I miss it. Especially the last time we hiked, chattering about baking for so long that we lost both the time and the trail, and had to find our way home in the dark. I can't think of a better person to get lost with, but I'll never have your touch for flour.

Who will hunt down the old Time-Life series cookbooks and save them for me? Who will bring a covered plate of her Thanksgiving meal, complete with chestnut purée, to my sick husband, while I eat mine far away with my family? Who will compliment my borscht, though I've never been to Russia and she has?

Who can talk as endlessly as I can about food and books?

Sally always set the right context for each meal, especially those eaten outside. There, she could slow down our urgent passion for food by coaxing the flavor out of simple ingredients. Our families' last picnic was a lunch of basic foods cooked on a stone grill provided by the state park. Her brood was the same configuration as mine, a husband and a toddler daughter. Our site was tucked among the trees next to the lake, but out of view. We shelled and munched peanuts, tossing the shells into the fire, while our meal cooked: split kielbasa squeezed together onto the grate, hot dogs for the kids, spongy buns and mustard, local corn, already lightly cooked, that we only had to re-heat to a smoky warmth. Even the ubiquitous August zucchini, skewered and marinated in lemon and oil, tasted right.

Sally learned her outdoor craft from a kind of Mosquito Coast dad. Each summer he marched his family of five girls deep into the woods, apart from the world, for almost four months. There were quirky rules at their campsite. No cutting of the girls' long tresses was allowed, and he held other views and habits peculiar and constraining. But, who knows? Maybe those isolated summers of endless rules, reading and campfire meals taught her to look toward the light, never the gloom, and nurture us all with her endless chatter of food, books, and more food. 'I'm not a Pollyanna', she used to say. But indeed, she worked hard at being one, and usually succeeded.

For our lakeside dessert Sally smuggled in a surprise for her husband's birthday: a homemade ring of her pound cake, hidden in a large Danish butter cookie tin. It appeared magically, filled with the last of her garden's raspberries, and topped with stay-alight candles. After our smoky lunch, her buttery dessert gave our meal the proper landing. And Sally knew her can of real, not fake, whipped cream would add a decadent touch.

At book group we competed. I made an understated olive oil cake with lemon and she countered with an almost-but-not-quite-too-bitter chocolate tart dotted with chocolate-covered coffee beans. I concocted effortless candies that I called 'Smooches', using premium bittersweet chocolate, spread ultra-thin and crowned with dried cherries. But she topped me with almond cookies, each dimpled with the raspberry jam made from her berry bushes out back. *Delicious*, everyone commented, not understanding how Sally and I played culinary catch-up.

For twenty years she was the sharpest fixture in that group. I took pleasure in her advocacy for authors, especially if books were difficult or unpopular. She intuitively understood an author's voice, the book's context and, perhaps most importantly, how each book filled a need. We ate our cake and sipped herbal tea, while Sally gave books eight out of ten just for being books; just because their authors had the courage to write them. She took the writer's side, identifying with whatever they needed to express: she pushed their case. That doesn't mean she liked everything indiscriminately – her thoughts on the remaining 8-10 spread were heavily nuanced.

Sally died after her second bout of cancer returned with a vengeance. It was just before the yellow Coltsfoot bloomed the following spring, though she insisted they were flowering outside the window from her hospital bed at home. Maybe it was the morphine, maybe just Sally's optimism. Weeks later, her husband invited me by to take what I wanted. Naturally, I headed into her kitchen, which was strangely silent. I didn't want anything, though I noticed she had a drawer of plastic tops, while at home I had all bottoms, no tops. I walked over to her fridge to open the door, though I knew its shelves well enough. They'd be jammed with her cook's tools: the chutney she'd made last fall, the orange marmalade that was never too sweet, along with fermenting and sugared five-sided glass jars, long unopened and filled with the mysteries that made for good eating.

Behind me, her two copper pots stood on the stove top, waiting. They were once filled with the borscht Sally had loved. It had been dense with vegetables and chunks of beef, Moscow borscht – I'd once read that Nureyev said it needed half a cow to complete. It didn't, but we'd laughed about that over that stove.

It's been years since. But just yesterday, Sally returned again, as my Great-Aunt Ida told me the dead tend to do. Just like that, while sharing a fat slice of carrot cake in our neighborhood café, before my husband could utter something sweet, but bland, like *Pretty Good, eh?*, Sally joins us. She's chattering as my fork presses down through the cake, releasing its play of cinnamon and nutmeg, with the right touch of allspice. It's a classic, we admit; we both love the classics, books and food. But, she isn't impressed with its crumb, nor am I. It's too dense, and we know it. Still, after a mouthful or two, we forgive the cake. Sally, because she tried to find the good, me because Sally's with me, as ever, pointing it out. **H**

11th March, Montmartre

by Connor Harrison

Walked, drifted, up to the top of Montmartre and
the Basilica. The artists in the square behind it,
peddling their work. I sat on the steps for a while
with Sacré-Cœur behind me, enjoying the sun.
A man playing a harp: 'My Heart Will Go On.'
At the end of each song everyone clapped, but
there was no money in his open case. A little later
he began to get irritated; I couldn't see what had
changed. He stood from his chair and left his
harp there on the steps, catching the light in its
strings. Further up was a man dressed and painted,
pretending to be a classical white statue. The harp-
player shouted in French and waved his arms, but
the statue, inevitably, ignored him. I was thinking
of the word crème, how it sounds better and more
satisfying than cream, how the r sticks like cream
in the mouth, the nearer m. How crème is closer to
what cream is. Fresh cream. Crème fresh.

By the time the man had returned to his harp, an immense black cloud was rolling in over the right-hand side of the city. But the sky on the left was still a spring blue so that, from my view, it looked as if the sky was closing. The clouds trailed their rain over the city – and a few minutes later reached above the Panthéon in the distance, and slowly gathered over the Basilica too, scattering perfect balls of hail. The crowds brought up their hoods and their umbrellas, and the harpist – cut off in the middle of a song – stuffed his instrument into its case. The men further down, with the bracelets and the shiny little Eiffel Towers, covered everything with red blankets. The rain and the hail fell for five minutes until, like a switch, it all stopped, and I stayed up there long enough to watch the clouds slip over the edge of Paris, out across the country. **H**

Ekphrasis

*From the Greek ἔκφρασις (ékphrasis), meaning 'description';
a work of art produced as a rhetorical exercise,
in response to another work, real or imagined.*

The Little Patch of Yellow Wall

by Kimmo Rosenthal

Sometimes one literary image is enough to transport us from one world to another...a thought cleverly hiding behind its images, lies in the shadow waiting for the reader.

– Gaston Bachelard[1]

Nowadays, most non-fiction essays tend to interrogate real-life experiences by exploring relationships, family history, and political or social events, with very few addressing experiences in the invisible world of our imagination. Some of the most profound such experiences are evinced by the act of reading or looking at art. Contemplating the work of others can inspire us in unique ways. There are instances when a literary or pictorial image allows us to see the world through new eyes, illuminating a landscape where a different consciousness reigns.

In one of the most memorable scenes from Proust[2], the author Bergotte stands – moments before his death – in front of Vermeer's *The View of Delft*, whereby he becomes transfixed by a patch of yellow on a wall in the painting, causing him to reflect on how he never became the writer he should have. How does one measure the meaning and value of an artistic existence? Bergotte finds himself lacking in terms of effort expended in honing and perfecting his writings (as we might all do).

> *I ought to have gone over them with a few layers of color, made my language precious in itself, like this little patch of yellow wall.*

On a 'celestial pair of scales', he weighs the meaning of his life against this patch of yellow. Had all of his cathectic efforts to achieve something of lasting value been worth it? Josef Czapski, in his luminous lectures on Proust[3], summarizes this with even greater eloquence than the original passage, asking a question that exercises all struggling writers and artists:

> *What could justify such an unremitting effort*
> *towards an end that probably no one will notice,*
> *or comprehend, or most likely even see?*

This question is unanswerable, although Proust finds justification in these unremitting efforts as an inevitable necessity – of being under the compulsion to attain something inaccessible, yet of indescribable personal importance. Like Proust, we find ourselves –

> *beneath the sway of those unknown laws which we*
> *obeyed because we bore their precepts in our hearts.*

For me, Bergotte's phrase 'language precious in itself' holds the key. I have come to believe writing is autotelic, in other words having a purpose in and not apart from itself. It has taken me quite some time to discover this. The act of writing primarily speaks to the writer. In discussing writing as a means of expressing oneself, Anne Carson says 'the point is not to find the reader, the point is the writing itself. It should become a gesture as private and accurate as her own name.'[4]

In Roberto Calasso's notion of absolute literature – a literature in search of absolutes, that refuses to be categorized or beholden to agreed-upon conventions – its language is recognizable by 'a certain vibration or luminescence of the sentence (or passage).'[5] This luminescence or vibration might open the door to an unbidden moment of revelatory insight. When we read or look at art, I believe we are all looking for our own little patch of yellow wall.

The art critic Peter Schjeldahl invoked Bergotte's death when writing about a similar epiphanic experience while looking at Vermeer's *Young Woman with a Water Pitcher*.[6] A patch of lapis-lazuli-tinted white on a headscarf is 'an illusion of reality more thrilling than any lived reality could be.' It is a moment of 'abrupt crystallization.'

As I read and write – for they form an inseparable diptych – I find myself looking for something exquisite to inspire me. The word exquisite seems apposite, I think, as it has its roots in the Latin 'exquirere', which means 'to search thoroughly.' I can recall occasions, not dissimilar to Schjeldahl's, when I have read something that has resulted in such a moment of abrupt crystallization.

The phrases that Writer uses in David Markson's wonderful *This Is Not A Novel* to describe the very work we are reading resonated with me profoundly: 'unclassifiable, erudite, filled with literary allusions, idiosyncratic, totally lacking in any appeal to the average reader.' While for many these descriptives might seem problematic, flying in the face of the prevailing winds, so to speak, I felt a profound sense of affirmation for my own writerly aspirations.

Also, an unimaginably exquisite sentence from Proust affected me like the little yellow patch of wall.

When on summer evenings the melodious sky growls like a wild animal and everyone grumbles at the

*storm, it is because of the Méséglise Way that I am
the only one in ecstasy inhaling, through the noise of
the falling rain, the scent of invisible, enduring lilacs.*[8]

It is perhaps my single favorite sentence, the epitome
of language precious in itself, possessing a supreme
beauty to strive for in writing.

I reread parts of Proust every year; one can open
to any page and become captivated and inspired.
I want to learn how to utilize the full richness and
expressiveness of language, with the same kind of
density and intricacy, imagery and insight, in order
to make my own 'private, accurate gesture', and
find my own 'miracle of pure style.'[9] I can only
hope that, in the admixture of foolish ambition
and blind hope, the merest trace or echo of such
a miracle might alight upon me and allow me to
produce my own little patch of yellow wall. **H**

1. Bachelard, Gaston. 'The Literary Image' in *Air and Dreams*. Translated by Edith R.
   Farrell and C. Frederick Farrell. The Dallas Institute Publications (1988)

2. Proust, Marcel. *The Captive and the Fugitive*. Translated by C.K. Scott Moncrieff and
   Terence Kilmartin. The Modern Library (2003), p244-6

3. Czapski, Josef. *Lost Time (Lectures on Proust in a Soviet Prison Camp)*. Translated by Eric
   Karpeles. New York Review Books Classics (2018). These remarkable lectures are from
   memory in a Soviet camp providing solace to his fellow prisoners.

4. Carson, Anne. *Float*. Knopf Publishing (2016). These phrases come from the pamphlet *Candor*.

5. Calasso, Roberto. *Literature and the Gods*. Translated by Tim Parks. Vintage (2002)

6. Schjeldahl, Peter. '*Vermeer*' from *Hot, Cold, Heavy, Light (100 Art Writings, 1988-2018)*.
   Abrams Press (2019)

7. Markson, David. *This is Not a Novel*. Counterpoint (2001)

8. Proust, Marcel. *Swann's Way*. Translated by Lydia Davis. Penguin (2002), p190

9. Hardwick, Elizabeth. *Sleepless Nights*. New York Review Books (2001). Elizabeth
   Hardwick used the phrase 'miracle of pure style' to describe Billie Holiday. I find
   Hardwick herself to be endowed with that miracle.

The Royal Society of Literature

RSL Giles St Aubyn Awards for Non-Fiction now open for submissions

The RSL is currently accepting submissions for the fifth year of the RSL Giles St Aubyn Awards for Non-Fiction.

Three awards – one of **£10,000**, one of **£5,000**, and one of **£2,500** – are offered to support writers to complete their first commissioned works of non-fiction by buying them time for writing or research.

Writers may submit themselves or their publishers or agents may submit on their behalf. The writer must be resident in the UK or Republic of Ireland.

These Awards present an extraordinary opportunity to realise the full potential of the book to come.

This year's judges are
Gwen Adshead, Clive Myrie and Fiona St Aubyn

The deadline for entries is 5pm on Friday 17 September.

SCAN ME

☛ **For more information and to enter the RSL Giles St Aubyn Awards 2021**

JOIN US

NEW FOR 2021!

Digital Events Pass
£25 a year

Attend all of our online events free of charge

RSL Membership
£50 a year*

RSL Young Person's Membership
(for under 30s)
£30 a year*

* Plus a £10 admin fee in the first year

- Attend all of our events free of charge
- Subscribe free to our magazine *RSL Review* and quarterly newspaper *Our Mutual Friend*
- Attend our online Book Clubs free of charge
- Take advantage of exclusive offers with our partner organisations
- Support our charitable aims as the national voice for the value of literature

rsliterature.org

The Promise of a Dinner Party

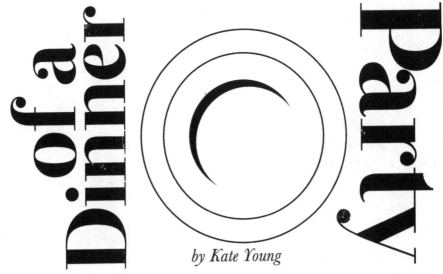

by Kate Young

I have always loved to eat. A career spent in catering kitchens and as a food writer didn't occur to me until my 30s, but I have been happily anticipating meal times (and each possible food time in between) for longer than I can remember.

I grew up surrounded by a sprawling extended family who invested their time and energy in meals, in shared time spent around a table. I was a lucky kid. The food on our plates sang so vividly of south-east Queensland: ripe mangoes, sausages cooked on the barbeque on the deck, summer rolls stuffed with prawns and glass noodles, hot lamb saagwala from the local Indian, mum's grilled lamb chops, flash fried local fish. What we ate at home was always delicious, even on a regular weeknight.

But I particularly loved the ritual when there were people round for dinner. Of setting out plates and cutlery and water jugs, of people gathered together at a table, of the candles burning low as guests sipped cafetière coffee and said 'oh go on then' in response to the offer of more dessert. I loved making a bit more of an effort than we would when it was just us.

The kitchen was the proverbial heart of our home, but it was only one half of it – the dining table was the other. At a push (and push we so often did), our dining table could seat sixteen, elbows bumping, conversations overlapping, barely enough space for our glasses and plates and all the platters that ran down the centre between us. During the school week, that table is where we'd make plans over breakfast, where we did our homework, where we gathered together in the evening. It was a piece of furniture that was mostly too big for the four of us, and so half of it was often covered with mum's patient files, with organised piles of opened bills and letters, with half-finished puzzles or board games. But underneath the tidy stacks lay the potentiality, the possibility. The promise of a crowded table, of people coming round for dinner.

It would be simplistic to say that I have been searching for a replacement to that dining table ever since. I have, of course I have. I've been longing for a room big enough to hold a long dining table since I moved out of my family home. But I moved to London just after the financial crash of 2008, and worked for free as an intern for a year.

I was lucky to have any living space in my shared flats; my dining tables over the next decade all had hinges, so they could be folded and tucked away when we needed the limited space to serve an alternative function. But it hardly mattered. It turned out that it was really the potentiality I've longed for, the promise of shared meals with people I love. And that's something I've found around all sorts of tables.

At 2am, after we'd been at a party, or out at the pub, I cooked the kind of thing we were all in dire need of: pesto pasta, cheese toasties, pancakes, ramen noodles

The first year I spent in London was in a flat above a bank, with mouldy walls and an electric blue carpet. I lived with a couple of guys I'd gone to university with, and we spent that first winter making our freezing flat cozy and welcoming. With three Australians in the house, our sofa often played host to some friend or other who was visiting; we brought elements from 'home' into our new shared home as often as possible. Whether we had guests, or it was just the three of us, we cooked together, our tiny galley kitchen affording us barely enough space to pass by one other, our dinners mostly eaten on the sofa so we could avoid the unsteady folding chairs.

It was in my next flat – the kitchen slightly bigger, with more than the single shelf in the under counter fridge that I'd had in the first flat – that I began cooking in earnest. My flatmate had the bedroom, and so my bed took up half the living room, a set of IKEA shelves filled with books the only suggestion of a line between where I slept and where we entertained. The coffee table was two long bench seats covered with a tablecloth that we whipped off when we were in need of seating. The dining table from my childhood home wouldn't even have fitted into the room.

There were well-planned dinner parties in that flat, but I mostly liked seeing it full of people in the early hours of the morning. In the evenings, it made sense to restrict guest lists to a number we could comfortably fit around the table: four, or six at a push. But with people perched on the sofa, on the bench seats, on the floor, I could feed twelve or so, cutlery set out in piles on a side table somewhere and bowls passed around until everyone had something in front of them. At 2am, after we'd been at a party, or out at the pub, I cooked the kind of thing we were all in dire need of: pesto pasta, cheese toasties, pancakes, ramen noodles.

I relished rare nights on my own in the flat, making elaborate meals for myself, trying out new recipes, playing with ingredients I couldn't afford when cooking for a crowd. But I loved being able to look around the living room and to imagine. I'd see those nights when there would be six of us around a table, or when it was just my flatmate and me eating together on the sofa, or when the whole room was filled with more people than we really had space for. I loved the promise of meals in the future, of planning menus with dear friends in mind, of knowing I'd have people around again soon.

I live on my own now, so it's something I've thought a lot about over the past year. My flat is in South Gloucestershire, overlooking the hills and valleys of Stroud. Much of the living space is dominated by a table large enough to seat – at a squash, a push, sixteen of us. But the promise of people coming round for dinner has been impossible, literally illegal, for more months in this past year than not. Bar a couple of back garden picnics with friends who have outdoor living space, I have eaten all my meals in the past five months alone. It's been so long since I've had people around my dining table that I worry I've forgotten the ritual of it, the flow of a good dinner party, the component parts that make an evening come together. There's a very real prospect that, the first time there are people at this table again, I'll be so overwhelmed that I'll retreat to the kitchen (my safe space, at crowded parties).

It might be a while, then, until I can ease myself towards inviting fifteen people to dinner. No matter, because there are plenty of other things I have missed too. Meals spent in the company of close friends, rich with potential and possibility and ritual, and all those things I love. There are so many things I've missed, so many that I want.

I want to wander into a restaurant on a whim. I want to snag a table or a couple of seats at the bar. I want to be pushed into a waiting area to sip on cocktails and lust over the menu, while we wait for a buzzer to vibrate on the table between us. I want to go and eat dim sum and order more steamer baskets than there's room on the table for, and then order a few more.

I want to walk home arm in arm with a friend, late at night, eating chips from the same spine-shudderingly squeaky Styrofoam box. I want to buy two scoops of ice-cream in a cone after a swim in the sea, and race to finish it before it melts down my arm. I want to walk into a market in another country, and leave with an ingredient I have never seen before. I want to order a drink that comes with a bowl of olives in the perfect shade of green. Or crisps seasoned with just the right amount of salt. Or some little local snack that's been dropped in hot oil and is still punishingly hot. I want to have more than three meals a day, because how will I try everything on my list otherwise?

I want to stand and watch someone I love in the kitchen – watch them make a cup of tea, or cook a steak, or fry an egg

I want to sit at a dear friend's dining table and pull meat from the carcass of a roast chicken, mopping up the juices in the pan with bread, our knuckles knocking together as we fight for the best bits. I want to stand and watch someone I love in the kitchen – watch them make a cup of tea, or cook a steak, or fry an egg. I want them to tell me they don't need help, that they've got it, that there's nothing I can do, that they just want me to keep them company.

I want to be at a wedding, two glasses of fizzy wine in, trying to make friends with the person holding the platter of canapés. I want to know there's a meal ahead that I had no hand in choosing, one that will be regularly interrupted by the tinkling of a fork against a glass, by achingly sincere speeches. I want to have two slices of wedding cake, knowing someone else has decided they're too full to properly enjoy theirs. I want to be seated next to someone I've never met, brought together only by our love of the people declaring their commitment to each other in front of us.

In order to manage the inevitability of over-catering when living alone, I have taken to leaving leftovers in take away food boxes outside my friends' doors

So often, these feel like frivolous asks. My adopted home is suffering the effects of a decade of austerity under a conservative government, and of deep cuts to public services. More than 8 million people in the UK are living in food poverty. Despite my loneliness, I know I am luckier than most; there have been good meals on my table in the past few months, and enough food in my fridge. Left to my own devices, it turns out I would basically live on eggs, greens, and toast, but I have had to continue testing recipes for work. I have spent the winter enjoying soups, stews, homemade dumplings and pasta. I have roasted chickens and perfected spring rolls and tested loaf after loaf of babka. In order to manage the inevitability of over-catering when living alone, I have taken to leaving leftovers in takeaway food boxes outside my friends' doors – a phone call and a wave as we stand a respectful distance apart alerting them to the presence of a meal on their doorstep.

And so I have eaten good food. But my gosh, I have missed having people round for dinner.

There's a song by The Highwomen that I've listened to a lot in the past year. A friend (whose Parisian living room I've spent so many evenings longing to journey back to) put it on a playlist for me. Every time it comes on while I'm running, or cooking, or walking through the green hills that I can see from my window, there's a line that makes me catch my breath – it's about a crowded table, about having enough space for everyone, about a house filled with people you love. It's all I've ever wanted. To have a place to bring people together, where I can build my own family, far from 'home'. It's the thing that has made this country, twelve thousand miles from where I grew up, feel like home too.

I know that for many of us – those who haven't lost jobs or homes or people in this relentlessly horrible year – things will soon return to some semblance of normality. But I know too that it's been an impossibly long time coming. That we have lost so much in the meantime, so much potential: human contact, family, time spent sharing a meal. And so I am reassuring myself, in what I hope are these final strange months, by the distant future in which there will be a crowded table. By the promise of people coming round for dinner. **H**

A Mind Full of Sake

by Edward Little

Delirious, I lowered my Turtle Beach headphones to my shoulders, cupping my ear to hear what he'd said. What? Japanese. Don't know why I expected anything else. Getting closer, I noticed his liver spots first, a constellation dotting from chin to forehead, then his gummy grin pulled me in with the handshake.

Ey, A-me-ri-ca? his tongue clicked, flicking out of his mouth on the ri.

Igirisu, I defended a little too quickly, not because I didn't like Americans, but I'd become borderline patriotic since leaving home.

Ah! Laughing in what I guessed was an imitation of Prince Phillip, he launched into speech, and even though I couldn't tell what he was saying, it somehow felt that he was starting from the middle of a story he was telling himself.

Ey, America! Nomu? He asked, cutting his sentence dead with a spasm of the neck.

After six months of teaching *I Can* and warning countless boys from saying *I fuck*, I needed a drink.

First strap, then second, he undid his gardening gloves before wiping his forehead and placing them on the edge of a plant pot. His home was a one-storey, like others in the area, but wooden pillars supported the structure rather than steel beams. A bonsai stood in front of his house, reaching out into the street – picturesque but with a studied, almost anime aesthetic, nature living hand in hand with its neighbours. I hadn't seen an untamed garden in months, this one was no exception, and my attention waned.

Then the old Japanese man ushered me into his house, flicking his tongue like he was trying to catch flies; and the sun was blocked out when the door shut behind me. Dark brown walls displayed a gallery of photos that seemed to lead to the kitchen; black and white frames of a wedding, slowly replaced with a boy in faded colour. I followed him into a kitchen, separated from the living room by a paper partition, the only light filtering through from a quiet TV on the other side. Hard to see the old man as his outline rummaged in a cupboard; he eventually smashed a glass and the partition door opened. It was then that she saw me.

I've yet to hear a woman scream so loud, and at first I thought it was directed at me, but by the time my ears had cleared, I learnt her husband's name as she twatted him over the head with a slipper.

Toru!

Maybe this isn't the first time he's brought someone home, I thought, as Toru defended himself against the tiny old lady with the kitchen brush.

Baka, she grumbled, shunning him with a wave of an arm as she retreated back to the television, closing her paper wall behind her.

I just stood there, politely smiling the whole time as I thought about making an exit, but he flashed a smirk. Pointing towards the front door, he led me back through the hall.

Beeru?

Beer?

Nodding, he confirmed the day wasn't over as the sun greeted us outside.

Disappearing for a minute, Toru returned with a paint-chipped bike from beside his house.

OK, OK, he said.

OK, I replied, trying to figure out what was going on, but by the time he'd leaned the bike onto me, he was off, shouting as he ran, and it took a few seconds to decide *screw it,* get my feet on the pedals, and give chase.

Following him through a web of neat roads, he weaved from side to side, waving reassurance to his retired neighbours as preparation for what they'd see next: a young British man pedalling in a tank top and suit pants, covered in tattoos, who'd more than likely taught one of their grandchildren. I was what my company called a *Super Sub,* for every elementary school in Ibaraki-Shi, and the sum of those commutes could be seen scarred into the bags of my eyes.

Coming to a stop, Toru swallowed, watching his own sweat hit the ground as he steadied his hands on his knees. I realised I knew the Family Mart he'd taken us to.

Opposite was Higashi Elementary, the school I'd been teaching in only two hours earlier.

Shit, sorry – Toru? I scrambled, but he'd marched ahead with his daydreams of beer. Parking the bike next to the store, two kids saw me, their identical yellow hats making them look like tiny builders.

Sensei?

Blazer, shirt, and tie, moist bundle at the bottom of my rucksack, were beyond recovery, but the dress code was underlined in my contract: Keep all tattoos covered. Sidestepping the aisles, I searched for Toru, like we were starring in a Japanese crime drama, but instead of robbing the place, we were avoiding children so that I could get pissed in front of a school that employed me. Eventually I found him holding four beers and a bottle of sake by the fridges.

Parking the bike next to the store, two kids saw me, their identical yellow hats making them look like tiny builders

Tired enough to ignore all reason, I followed him to the till.

Fami chiki, Toru said, putting the alcohol on the counter. The server, pimpled with messy black hair, repeatedly caught himself from looking up at us, an odd pairing he didn't expect to see, as he bagged the drinks — and a box of fried chicken.

Thank you, I said, simply to watch the cashier smirk, a small blush giving a deeper shade to his acne.

Walking to the bench outside, we sat opposite the school. The building was a creamy white and the setting sun still illuminated half of the front wall. I searched the windows for silhouettes, but the classrooms appeared dark: no kids to be seen.

It's a beautiful day, I commented, taking two beers from the bag and handing one to Toru. Nodding, he fingered open the tab, taking a greedy swig in a way that reminded me of someone I used to call

Dad. The liquid caused the loose skin of his throat to wobble like a wave.

Oishii. Delicious, he said.

Kampai. Cheers. I raised my can and, with a laugh, we clinked tins. I tried to use Google Translate as we drank our beers, but Toru waved away my attempts to communicate with a smack of his tongue against the roof of his mouth. It was the school he watched, scanning the rooms that were full earlier, click, click, clicking his tongue, like he was trying to echolocate someone lost in the building.

The beer was good, the chicken even better. Toru touched none of the food, instead starting on the sake, and I realised how hungry I was. Whatever anxiety I had disappeared with the alcohol, and sucking clean the final chicken bone, licking the oil from my fingers, I listened as Toru started to talk. Slowly at first, hands outstretched, half grasping like he was picking the words from mid-air, he found his rhythm, sentences so unfamiliar to my ear that they sounded like spells. I'd fill quiet moments with empty words because silence makes me paranoid, yet the more he spoke, the easier it felt just to exist there, drunk on the idea of what he might be telling me, and to allow the excess of everyone I'd ever met to fill my senses. Their noise. Their smell. Their crowding. Their ability to fill up too much space. With the sun almost set – Toru started to weep.

Sumimen, he sniffled, pinching at his eyes and rising to his feet, as the alcohol rushed red through his cheeks, animating an embarrassment I'm sure he felt. As he was about to leave, the realisation that

Toru had already become a memory was enough for my eyes to glaze over.

I watched him run, a sloppy stride which had his leg over the bike and on the pedal by the time I struggled together with the leftover chicken bones.

Arigato! I shouted, feeling silly but happy to give weight to my dramatics, waving at him with the bottle of sake he'd abandoned. *Sayonar-*

Thank you, he said, one shoe on the ground, head facing west, like an echo from the other side of the world in a city that's always raining. Prepared to say something else, mouth paused open and a low cry grumbling in his throat, he swallowed, pedalling his bike away until it disappeared between the maze of roads.

Night crept in warm, a row of crows cawing on the school gate a hint that maybe I should go home. Instead, I took the bottle to the park, drinking on a swing designed for a child, and calling friends in England to talk about Toru – what we'd done, debating the content of his tear-inducing monologue, which by midnight had inspired in us countless fantasies of who he was: a drunk, a spy, a romantic; an endless thread of possibilities that I could forever retell in cafés, train stations, and bars.

With a belly full of chicken and a mind full of what that day had been, I stumbled to my apartment, the scenery coming back into focus. **H**

The Slow Dance

by Pragya Agarwal

QUICHE. Quickee? Quickey? I roll the words around my mouth as I spell the letters out in my head. Qui-kay? I read it aloud in my head, pausing uncertainly as I stare at the menu board. I don't know what that means. I look at the vast array of things laid out in front of me, vegetables that seem very unfamiliar to me, with names that I have never heard before. The heat from the counter and the lamps is rising up my face and through my thick coat — a coat I had bought in a sale from that shop called Debenhams, a dull brown colour, two sizes too big hiding the emptiness around me. The server behind the food counter looks at me impatiently. There is a long line already building:

the lunch queue in our refectory every day at 1pm. I remember that I haven't had anything to eat since I woke up, and my stomach is rumbling. I feel faint. My blood sugar is falling. It always happens to me when I haven't eaten for a long time. I cannot faint here with all these students milling around me. I gaze up at the enormous ceiling; it is like nothing I have seen before, very high with wooden beams.

'Are you going to have anything, love?' the server asks again, frustration written deep in his voice and on his face. I don't know what I can eat, I say to myself. I pretend to look closely at the board again over the counter where all the dishes and their prices are listed. I don't know how all this works. I don't know how much all this will cost me. Maybe I will just have a cup of tea. That seems straightforward enough. I mentally calculate the cost of a cup of tea: £3.50. So, what is that in rupees? I am good at mental maths but anxiety is making thoughts and numbers swim and jumble around in my head. 1 pound is around 80 rupees, so that is roughly around 280 rupees. 280? For a cup of tea? What are they going to give you? Gold leaves? I imagine what my father would say if he were here.

'Oh, I am OK,' I say quickly and move on, my face flushed and embarrassed, imagining everyone laughing at me behind my back. It is OK. I can get through the day. I will pick something up on the way back.

—

I am standing in front of the supermarket shelves with a small basket in my hands. I am here with some of my housemates, joining their weekly trip to the local supermarket 30 minutes walk from where we live. It is freezing, and my toes and shoes were wet before we were even halfway here. Soggy toes, frosty stares. I should have bought some better shoes, I think to myself. But these seemed like the best shoes back in Delhi. On the dusty back streets of Sarojini Nagar, when the heat and dust mingled together. It was 25 degrees Celsius even though it was winter. I had never been to the UK. I had never been anywhere outside India. Actually, I lie. I had been to Nepal, to Kathmandu and to Pokhara, which is when I flew in an aeroplane for the very first time. Kathmandu seemed just like a slightly different version of India, though. Not very different, almost too similar.

I pick up some things that sound familiar. Rice, of course. Pasta, yes I have had it once or twice but only in restaurants.

I stare at the shelves in front of me, in this small town very far up in the north of England. I pretend that I understand it all, while my brain is doing that flippy-floppy thing again where things move in and out of focus. They scatter in an untidy heap, as I try to fit the pieces around and around, probing different configurations. One has to make sense. One has to be the one that seems like something. One has to be the one where I fit. My housemates — from the Netherlands, Belgium, and England —

flit around rapidly like zooming figures on skates, helter and skelter, picking up this and that, their eyes not even going to the shelves but their fingers already knowing where things are. They fit in here. I try to pretend that I do. I pick up some things that sound familiar. Rice, of course. Pasta, yes I have had it once or twice but only in restaurants. It should be straightforward enough. Bread, jam, butter. They are things that match the patterns in my head, those templates that we carry around, shaped by our experiences and memories, our mental models of the world that we use to make sense of it. These match, but with a jarring edge, as if trying to squeeze into a jumper that is quite not their own. The arms and neck go in, but then it floats around the body, hanging loose waiting for something that is missing.

—

I had arrived in London Heathrow very late at night on a British Airways flight. My very first flight outside the Indian subcontinent. There had been fog in Delhi and flights were delayed for several hours. By the time I had landed and gone through immigration, proving that I had a right to be here – all the paper evidence of my scholarship from the British Council, bank statements, visa – it was 1am. These hundreds of papers carefully and painstakingly arranged in a thick plastic folder to demonstrate that I existed; an attempt to prove that I would fit in, I would exist quietly, causing no disruption to the carefully stacked up pieces of many different lives here. The immigration officer stared at me, and then back at the visa again; we were there for almost an hour. My eyes were drooping. I had not eaten much on the plane and the hollowness in my middle was beginning to expand.

The officer asked: 'Have you brought pickles or any other food in your suitcase? Most people from your country do.'

No, I had not. Even though my mother had carefully arranged those jars on the table in the days before I was due to leave. I had suddenly felt ashamed of them, as if they wouldn't fit in with my life in England, even as I wanted to absorb them into my bloodstream before I left. But she had insisted in stashing a few packets of lentils in my suitcase.

'Who knows what you can get there?', the lines of her forehead deepening every day.

'Ma, it is a huge country. I am sure there will be everything easily available'.

My heart was wobbling but I had laughed at her. Now my luggage hadn't arrived, still stuck somewhere over the land and the oceans, those 4500 miles that I had just crossed.

There was no one from the British Council to welcome me, of course. I found a taxi somehow, asked them to take me to a hotel. I had sat at the edge of my seat, terrified as the taxi zoomed through the empty roads to a small bed and breakfast. I had smiled and nodded when the taxi driver told me that his favourite dish was chicken tikka masala.

I was shown to a tiny one-bed room with a sink in the corner. I was told that it would be 35 pounds for one night. I silently handed over the cash that I had carried with me from Delhi in a pouch hidden under my large blue and black waterproof jacket. I am surprised you are still alive, a friend tells me as I recount this story a few years later.

'Vegetarians eat fish and eggs, don't they?' the kind lady asked me, looking confused. I shook my head

At breakfast, there were many people. Nice people, lovely people, kind people. People who were sorry for the small brown girl all alone and lost. People who asked many questions about what I would eat, and what I like to eat. People who marvelled at my English.

'What would you like to ask for breakfast, love?', they asked me, and I realised that I hadn't eaten anything for more than 48 hours. I told them that I was vegetarian.

'I am sure we can work something up for you. Don't worry.'

My stomach rumbled, and I tried to make myself even smaller in case anyone heard. They brought me some fish, eggs and toast. The browns and yellows on the beige plate were making my eyes water, the smell rising from the fish were filling up my head, or maybe it was hunger.

'Vegetarians eat fish and eggs, don't they?' the kind lady asked me, looking confused.

I shook my head, smiled gratefully at her, and started picking at the food quietly, turning it over with my fork, pushing in a mouthful to assuage some of the gnawing hunger. I felt like I was being watched and I kept feeding the immense sense of gratitude: for the food, and for being allowed in here where I clearly did not belong.

—

The size of the supermarket makes me feel so small, as if I am a tiny mortal speck of dust in our vast universe. I look across the long aisles and try to map the miles back home to India. I see rows and rows of tinned vegetables: peas, carrots, onions, beans. All encased in metal containers of similar size and shape, except the colourful pictures and fonts on the labels. There is no way to tell which tin is better than another, which one has more flavour or more fragrance. My mother and I used to walk over to our local vegetable market most evenings. She with her cotton bag and a small shopping list written

There is no way to tell which tin is better than another, which one has more flavour or more fragrance

in pen, in the scribbly writing that she was often ashamed of. The list was carefully stored in her little handbag along with her monthly allowance. My mother and I didn't agree on many things. Most things. But we walked slowly, finding our way through the crowds, folding in and spreading out along the street, where vendors would set up their stalls with fresh vegetables picked from farms on the edges of the sprawling urban suburbs. The noise was often deafening and so we communicated with unspoken words. There was no space for argument, for disagreement, for conflict. Instead we worked together with a patented rhythm, moving in and out, zig and zag, touching and prodding the fruit and vegetables, smelling them to find those with the most flavour, then negotiating and haggling with the vendor. It was expected, and accepted. I learnt it there.

Those were the most enjoyable moments of my day, as my feet became soaked in dust from the streets, and I was marinated with the dripping humidity. Even as my body felt consumed, my heart and mind devoured this sensory overload, thinking hungrily of the dishes my mum would be cooking that day, and the rest of the week. We did not talk much as we walked back together, but I never felt closer to her than at those times.

Most days we sat in the tiny kitchen on the floor, all three sisters, while she made fresh parathas at the small stove on the counter. The kitchen had a tiny window that opened onto an internal courtyard. There was not much ventilation, and we would all be cramped onto a single mat on the floor, squeezed in together, knees and elbows folded around us, talking over each other, crashing mid-sentence. That was the only time we did talk. I was able to forget any grudges I had against my little sister, and she forgot how annoying she found me. We folded up parathas, eating with our fingers, scooping up subzi and achar, sometimes dividing one paratha into four, forcing our mum to eat while she cooked. We always ate more than we should have done, more than we needed. No one counted the dough as it disappeared under my mum's deft fingers. The house, and the kitchen, filled up with cooking smells and our loud chatter. I have never felt so full since, and my dark brown coat hangs even looser around me.

———

The lentil packets have burst in the suitcase somewhere along the way, and tiny orange and yellow pieces have sneaked into every nook and cranny of my clothes. I shake everything out carefully but keep finding these reminders in the pockets of coats and jackets: reminders of my mum's furrowed forehead, and her anxious hugs as I left India all those weeks ago. And every time I throw one of them away, I feel like a part of me and my home is drained away along with tiny pieces of my mother's heart.

I cry as I think of this, lying in bed wrapped in a duvet and a blanket, but the cold is seeping right through me even as I try to sleep in two jumpers and three pairs of socks. I wonder if the cold will make my tears freeze, and this thought cheers me for a short while.

'Cook curry for us!', my housemates demand every time we have a party. I don't know what a curry is really. There are all sorts of subzis. I decide I will just adapt one that I have eaten in the local 'Indian' curry house, adding pineapple to it as they do even though it sears my eyes, making me feel that I am rapidly driving myself further and further from home.

I tell them it is my grandmother's recipe. My grandmother will never know.

'Cook curry for us', my housemates demand every time we have a party. I don't know what a curry is really

Every night I call my little daughter up from the one public phone in the long corridor of our shared student house, the cord stretching across the thousands of miles. I sit in a cold and draughty corridor, my daughter in my parents' house back in India, where she will be until I can bring her here with me, until I can afford to be whole again. Every night I cry thinking of her. Every night I smile because she has told me about the food that she has eaten that day, about the paranthas she has eaten in my mother's kitchen. Sometimes I read to her from the new cookery book I have bought in a sale. And I promise to cook a new dish for her next time I am back in India, next time we can hug and hold each other close.

I rush around the kitchen between classes, trying to cobble together something to eat from the leftovers in the fridge. A few slices of bread, and some cold pasta. Maybe I can get some spread from the fridge. I find a small bottle that contains white sauce. It looks benign. One of my housemates must have bought it as part of our shared grocery shop. I

am in a hurry. The name means nothing to me. I
scoop out a big dollop and smear it on the bread;
shoving a huge bit in my mouth, gnashing it down
quickly as I hear the seconds tick louder and louder.

That day, she is asked to show her lunch for inspection by the school nurse ... I am a little confused. Is this normal school practice?

The explosion hits my head before my mouth can
process it at a visceral level. There is no sense of
beginning or end to this pain — it is a tsunami of
fire. I lie on the floor with my head in my hands. I
roll around on my back trying to imagine what it
would be like to live longer. I sit up and lean against
the counter, hugging myself tightly and telling
myself that it will be OK. Again and again. I am
not sure though. I am not sure what damage I have
done to myself. Those seconds ticking by seem like
an hour. I have been terrified of horseradish sauce
ever since.

—

My daughter is eight and she has just joined me in the
UK, now that I have a full-time job and can afford
to rent an apartment. She does not like the lunches
at school. She thinks they have no flavour and a
strange texture. I carefully prepare her packed lunch,
and inform the school that she will be bringing food
from home. Every morning I wake up early before
getting ready for work, before waking her up, and
julienne the different vegetables, carrots, broccoli,

spring onion, peas – she loves the colours – to make noodles for her lunch box. That day, she is asked to show her lunch for inspection by the school nurse.

'Mumma, she wanted to know if it is healthy food.'

I am a little confused. Is this normal school practice?

'She said that you people eat a lot of unhealthy food and so she is worried.'

I call the school to ask, but am nervous about making a fuss.

'Oh, we want to make sure all the students are eating healthily,' they repeat. I am not sure what it is all about, but now I start worrying that I am overreacting, that I am being oversensitive. Now, every morning, as I am preparing the lunchbox, I feel like I am being watched, and I feel rage simmering inside me.

A magazine is doing a profile on me. They are sending a photographer over, they tell me, and wouldn't it be nice if I cook some food, get some photographs with the family. I make our favourite dishes: some fattoush, roasted vegetable couscous, and a tagine. I bring out our beautiful terracotta dishes that we had bought in the old markets in Egypt, Morocco and Cyprus, all blue and gold, with the intense sunny yellow that reminds me of the sunflowers in the Tuscan fields. The photographer takes one look at this spread and then back again at me.

'I didn't know you knew all this food,' she says in a deadpan manner, then laughs at her own joke.

———

One Christmas it snows, and the local canal freezes over. We walk tenderly from one end to the other, my new husband and my teenage daughter all holding hands, just the three of us. We are having the whole family over to ours for the first time. My in-laws, all five of them. They offer to bring food. I insist that they will have a traditional Christmas meal like they are used to. I research traditional recipes, old-fashioned processes, historic Christmas fayre through online archives, and old cookbooks that I unearth in second-hand bookshops. It is as if I will be able to understand where my husband comes from, and make sense of the threads that criss-cross us, and have drawn us together. It becomes an obsession, while my husband looks on, baffled.

'We can just buy things from the supermarket, you know', he says again and again, as if I am unable to comprehend this simpler way of doing things. I don't want shortcuts. They never get us anywhere. We might bypass distance, but it will catch up with us somehow, one day. Turkey brined for many hours, bread sauce with many complex steps, the cake that has to be fed every night for weeks. I want to know how slowness can also move us forward.

Sometimes we might appear to be standing still, but we can still surge through. It is the rhythm of our marriage, the slow dance that we do everyday between assimilation and fitting in. ◫

epoch ✕ press

Truth in Ink.

"ROOTS"
Available 1 August, 2021

As the world shifts and changes under social
and environmental pressures, 'Roots' harkens to
where we came from and what might ground us.
It is a collection of art that spans the globe and
the spectrum of human experience.

www.epochpress.org

Pork
Pra

Belly yer

by Maya Osman-Krinsky

On the eve of Super Tuesday, I leaned against a wall on Calle de los Libres, wiping crispy pork skin out of the corners of my mouth. My tongue, tingling from habanero, worked to dislodge a fleck of cilantro from between my two front teeth. It was far past dark, but the fluorescent strips on the food truck's ceiling sputtered every now and then, lighting the jolly vinyl humanoid pig that waved at customers from a plastic banner suspended over the prep-station. The vehicle illuminated the otherwise empty sidewalk, an old TV buzzing music videos from the aughts in the corner. A flame rose from behind the stainless-steel counter, licking four pairs of forearms and reddening the faces of the taqueros inside.

We stood at El Lechoncito de Oro, clutching foam trays of suckling pig taquitos with chicharrón, poring over the little plastic cups of salsa verde, salsa roja, and blow-your-mouth-off salsa especial that lined the counter. I was there with Rachael, a friend I'd made on a walking tour of Mercado Central de Abastos, one of the few markets in the city I hadn't explored on my own. She'd called me on WhatsApp asking if I wanted to run errands with her, and we met at a bar for a cocktail shortly after I'd replied to say yes. We wove in and out of mezcalerías in the city's center for hours, until, buzzed and hungry, we slumped in the shadow of Lechoncito's metal frame and ate until we could no longer feel our tongues.

That night was the penultimate Monday of the ten weeks I had spent studying in Oaxaca, Mexico. During that time, I was fortunate enough to encounter tastes and smells, textures and temperatures, songs and silences that exceeded the bounds of my comfortable descriptors, forcing me out into a new lexicon brilliant with specificity. Despite my familiarity with the Mexican culinary traditions found in the States, Mexico's food culture felt entirely novel. Oaxaca's food systems are uniquely part of the city's fabric in a way that I've felt viscerally in so few other places, and not without reason – Oaxaca is known as the food capital of Mexico. Oaxaca's indigenous past and present is a salient feature of the state and its cuisine: to this day, sixteen different ethnic groups continue to live in the place formerly known as Huaxyacac, the Nahuatl name for the land. Oaxaca's seven kinds of complex mole, iconic tlayudas, funky huitlacoche, sour chapulines, crunchy chicatanas, smoky pasillas, and countless uses of maize speak to this – if you're an attentive eater, you can't help but internalize Oaxaca's past and present. In short, there is a connection in Oaxaca with the land and the flavors and the sun that you cannot find anywhere else. That's paraphrasing an offhand comment made by Erica, a Chiapan-turned-Oaxaqueña, a mezcalera I met with Rachael.

That night was sardine-packed with stories, each one sliding up against the next, leaking funk and flavor into its neighbors

That night was sardine-packed with stories, each one sliding up against the next, leaking funk and flavor into its neighbors. Stories were an enormous part of my time in Mexico: I'd learned about the Olmecs' colossal heads, about Zapotec and Isthmian writing systems, about La Malinche and the skewed retellings of Cortes's arrival to the Americas. I'd read legends of the Virgin of Guadalupe and the forced conversion of the Incas, accounts of political corruption and voter fraud, of the construction of a Walmart a stone's throw from Teotihuacan, of NAFTA and the border crisis. But through all of these, the stories that stuck with me like the adobe-red soil on the soles of my shoes were about food. Rachael and I spoke about cuisines lost due to colonization and genocide, the ways in which language and food can be preserved side-by-side,

and how recipes change as they crawl from the
outskirts of a city closer to its center.

Still, embedded in the thrill I felt walking
through the buzzing streets and smoky markets
of Oaxaca was a greasy discomfort; despite
my American-student-abroad eagerness, the
tumultuous relationship between Mexico and
the US was constantly in the back of my mind. I
wanted to experience the tastes and smells of the
country without being the oily foreign consumer, a
superficial tourist, a voyeuristic intruder. I wanted
to free myself of implication and seek refuge in the
realm that I felt the most connected to – I wanted
badly for food to act as the salve, the connective
tissue, the equalizing force in a parasitic political
relationship. I wanted something soothing; even
though so much of this regional food was new to me,
I felt a depth to the culinary experience in Oaxaca
that I'd only felt in my own family's home cooking.
Sure enough, Middle Eastern and Polish influences
were present from Puebla to Guanajuato, crypto-
Jewish recipes were in use in modern Mexican
restaurants, and the worldwide fermentation fads
that had crept down to Oaxaca were met by those
that already existed – and in fact originated – in
Mexico's indigenous foodways.

Erica had commented about Oaxaca's land,
food, and sun as Rachael and I sat in her living
room with two thousand pesos worth of mezcal laid
out precariously on a wicker table in front of us.
Erica explained the production and origin of each
one – the kind of agave used, the soil properties,

the climate in the region – while Rachael squinted at the labels. We commented appropriately on the nose of the first mezcal, on the roundness and smoothness on the palette. It was doubtlessly a performance on my part, knitting my eyebrows over the tiny glass in my hand, swishing it dramatically from cheek to cheek, letting the smokiness coat my tongue. On how the mezcal opened on the second sip, the notes of sea salt and soil hitting the back of the throat after the last contraction of my esophagus post-swallow. We did the same for the second bottle, a little greener and more lactic, fiery in a way that stayed in my cheeks and hugged my teeth. Perhaps by the end it was earnest.

In the lulls between tastings, the conversation shifted from agaves to tepache, a fruit-based alcohol made from pineapple skins, peel from a plátano macho, and piloncillo, or cane sugar. Left to ferment in a vat with water for several days, the result is a tart and fizzy liquid, an ecosystem-specific elixir. Having dreamt of starting a fermentation dungeon somewhere in my off-campus Chicago walkup, I asked again about the process, already trying to map my route to collect the ingredients once I got home. Erica turned to me and shook her head, smiling. *You can't make it the same way in the States. My friends up there will call me after trying and say 'Erica, I have a jug of sweet water! What have I done wrong?' It's the problem of the globalized world, I tell them.* She explained that in the importation of Mexican fruit to North American markets, the washing process eliminates a lot of the wild yeasts necessary for tepache's fermentation process. As she poured the last of the three glasses of mezcal, Erica continued with a shrug: *There is just some special magic here.*

She warned us, as we each raised the short glass to our nose, then our lips, that we'd be tempted to name the flavor immediately

The third pour was not mezcal but comiteco, the liquor from a single distillation of pulque. Pulque is fermented aguamiel, the sap, or more literally, honey water, found at the center of maguey comiteco, a specific kind of agave. She warned us, as we each raised the short glass to our nose, then our lips, that we'd be tempted to name the flavor immediately. She asked us to sit with it for a moment in our heads, rather than our tongues: *taste this with an open mind, with a lot of thought.* Refraining from categorizing comiteco was a difficult task, but not impossible. It was an exercise for us, two earnest gringas whose home country meddled in the place we were calling a temporary home, whose home country turned economies, environments, and people on their heads on both sides of a border originally meant to prevent invasion from the North. Erica explained to us that comiteco's categorization is in the process of evolution. It is not mezcal or tequila or pulque, but a unique result of exhaustive research, precise heating and cooling processes, and quality control of wild yeasts. Comiteco comes from Chiapas, Mexico's southernmost state, and originated centuries ago, before heirloom ferments were considered

stylish. Like mezcal, the geographic origin is what
distinguishes the beverage from others of its kind;
the maguey plants don't only stand for agriculture,
but also symbolize the history, culture, and identity
of Chiapas. Resisting the instinct to contextualize
this unfamiliarity in and against what we knew
was the absolute least we could do. Expanding our
categories, or maneuvering around them altogether,
helped us engage in some informal reverence
towards a flavor intimidating in its namelessness,
defiant in its exquisite familiarity.

Like mezcal, the geographic origin is what distinguishes [comiteco] from others of its kind; the maguey plants don't only stand for agriculture, but also symbolize the history, culture, and identity of Chiapas

A lot of these flavors – comiteco, atole,
chapulines, nopales – I'd never encountered in
Chicago or New York, cities in which I spend the
most time, and both with significant Mexican
populations; but it didn't mean they weren't there.
Rather, it meant that I hadn't looked hard enough.
Last year, *Eater Magazine* had published a feature
on the 'United States of Mexican Food', explaining
the rise of the distinct Mexican cuisines that have
developed in the States. These 'American-Mexican
foodways' (named as such, even though Mexico
is in the Americas) act as vehicles of new regional
delicacies, but also as forces of culinary assimilation;
food critics and Mexican food aficionados alike
struggle with their claims to legitimacy. There
remain 'authentic' spots for purists: a famous Philly

barbacoa shop, in-house maize nixtamalization at D.C. restaurants, and even 'Puebla York', a community of Poblanos in East Harlem, serving cemitas, tacos de guisado, and chiles en nogada.

But another layer of difficulty arises when considering Mexican food interpreted by white chefs, who are largely men acting as keepers to 'foreign' flavors, connoisseurs of cultures and cuisines that are not their own. Rooted, artisanal foods are elevated to art, and priced accordingly. Even as this trend has come to Mexico, with Mexican chefs reinterpreting their cuisine to cater to tourists (as most 'fine dining' does), there is something that rankles like a rotting onion when the circle closes, as it does at El Destilado. The restaurant, on Calle 5 de Mayo — steps away from one of the main squares in Oaxaca Centro — is the 'brainchild of two young guys from the U.S.' who became 'enamored' with Mexican food and ingredients and set up a tasting-menu restaurant whose advertising almost suggests that they know how to serve Oaxacan food better than Oaxacans do. The issue of haute Mexican cuisine is complicated and, frankly, is not in my wheelhouse. Nevertheless, it's a problem of capitalizing through claims to authenticity and refinement from a globally dominant vantage point. It begs an inspection of the split between the perceived timelessness of culinary arts, and the rootedness of food that is actually artisanal, not just branded as such.

So far, this arrogance hasn't reached the carts that line the city's streets with flames and flickering lights after dark. I started home once Rachael and

I had licked our fingers, and exchanged promises to keep in touch while she figured out a move to Mexico City to work for Gabriela Cámara, a chef who had 'transfigured Mexico City's restaurant world' (Eater, again). As I walked the twenty minutes along Calzada de la República from the taco stand to my homestay, I counted my steps and shoved my hands into my pockets, suddenly cold. The dogs were howling maniacally like they did every night, and I picked up the pace, zigzagging from sidewalk to sidewalk on Calle Almendros, heart beating in my ears. It was past midnight, but my host mom, Evelia, was still awake when I loosened the bolt of the front gate and pushed the door open with the toe of my shoe. *¿Como se fue? ¿Tomaste, no? ¿Mezcal? Ah… Paloma* (she rarely called me by the right name) *descanse. Les sirvo el desayuno a las nueve, como normal.* I walked the short flight of steps upstairs and collapsed backwards onto my bed, eventually falling into a full, contented sleep.

This story gets stuck in the past tense; a night I've thought about nearly every day since. Each time, the details get diluted and the recollection of the spice lining my tongue fades. It was supposed to be a story about tacos al pastor, the sweating streetlamp dripping grease from the roasting slabs of meat onto corn tortillas, and about the bright pink gelatinas de nicuatole that sat on our breakfast table every Sunday morning. It was supposed to be about the Jewish conversos in Guadalajara, about the Polish refugees to Chihuahua and Nuevo León during World War II, about how diasporic

populations have so much in common, and how
we can still taste the traces they leave. But it is
not that — I have to wrench this story out of the
past tense because its relevance now is something
I can't romanticize with comparisons to my own
home. There is no way to separate the personal
from the political, no way to isolate the food I so
admire in Mexico from the land that has been
exploited by the country I reluctantly call home.
There is no ignoring the politics of consumption,
the literal and metaphorical internalizing of what
this home, this city, this country had to offer. There
was such extreme irresponsibility in imagining
that the disappointing and potentially disastrous
Super Tuesday outcome could be, in any way,
disconnected from where I was at that moment.

¿Como se fue? ¿Tomaste, no? ¿Mezcal? Ah... Paloma (she rarely called me by the right name) descanse. Les sirvo el desayuno a las nueve, como normal

My notebook from Mexico is so thick with
sketches and receipts, business cards, tickets and
to-do lists, that I am worried that despite any effort
at cataloging the day-by-day, I won't be able to do
justice to how complicated it feels to be someone
from the US in this exact intersection of space
and time. It is an identity heavy with politics and
baggage that is foreign in some ways and deeply
personal in others. I try to shed the skin I have
in the game by wriggling into a different one —
to claim my space in the story as a descendant
of a people who cross-pollinated with the ones

here, who were also physically, politically, and geographically traumatized. But to be vulnerable to the intersections of our stories, I have to interrogate my facts and my fictions, my numbness and my complacency, my experiences and my desires, my luxury of separating the personal from the political. I have to ask myself how I am related to the governments who had a hand in this, how much I take the hegemony of the Ziploc bag or the United Fruit Company for granted, how much I lean on my earnest bilingualism and guilt as a way out.

I thought I could soften this story like hominy in a food processor, pulsing it again and again with electric shocks until I could rub the color-drained granules between my fingers and see them dissolve. But this story needs hydration more than it needs me, it needs to steep in a rainstorm of honesty and of accountability. I was disappointed that food could and would not be the great equalizer in this story. There is too much thievery for that. I learned that though you can taste and learn a place, it does not mean you should blindly consume it. In trying to remember and recount the night I spent with Rachael and Erica letting our mouths meld with our minds, I'd understand the tension between the story I wanted to tell and the story I had to tell, the gap between my aspirational fictions and the guilt-streaked facts. I don't know where to go from here but I know it will depend on the bricks, on the corn, on the pigs and the water and the sky. I hope it will go up. ∎

Online self-guided creative writing courses

Enrol now!

- Study online at any time from anywhere
- Progress at your own pace with bite-sized chapters
- Free and paid-for courses available
- Gain confidence, increase productivity and learn new techniques
- Designed by experienced writers

courses.nationalcentreforwriting.org.uk

N National Centre for Writing

84 Hinterland ⎯⎯⎯⎯⎯⎯⎯⎯⎯⎯⎯⎯⎯⎯

On Meat

by Andrew Kenrick

Recipe for Apician Ofellae: Bone [the meat], roll up, tie it and put it in the oven. After it has been browned, take it out and dryroast it on a gridiron over a gentle fire so that it gives of its juices, without letting it burn. Pound pepper, lovage, sweet rush, cumin, liquamen, and flavour with passum. Put the ofellae in a pan with this sauce. When they are cooked, take them out, drain the sauce from them, sprinkle with pepper and serve. If they are fatty, take the skin off when you bind them up. It is also possible to make ofellae of this kind from belly pork.

– Apicius, 7.4.2[1]

The knife cuts through the carcass with ease. The blade is so sharp that the smallest amount of pressure easily parts flesh from bone. My brow furrows, as I concentrate on slicing the meat and not my hand. It would be too easy to slip, to lose a finger. I work slowly, carefully, remembering what I have just been taught about butchering a pig. How to cut the carcass into its primal cuts, the four key joints of meat from which other cuts are subsequently taken: shoulder, loin, belly and leg. It is the belly joint that I am after, although no part of this pig will go to waste; not even the head.

The name 'primal cut' is apt: there is something primitive about this practice. Man, blade and beast, cutting and carving the spoils of the hunt, just as we have done throughout history. The only difference is that, the further down the years we have come, the more removed from the act of butchery we have grown. We no longer see how living creature and packaged meat relate.

It's out of a desire to reconnect with what I eat – coupled with my research into the history of Roman cookery – that leads me, one cold Saturday morning, to be standing over a dead pig, knife in hand. I've come to the Marsh Pig, a charcuterie in Claxton, Norfolk that specialises in producing bacon, along with salami, chorizo, jerky and sausages. The Marsh Pig is run by Jackie and Sarah, who greet me with a bacon bap – homemade bacon, of course – and a mug of tea. The pig carcass is not their doing, however, but the butcher's. Richard has been a butcher since leaving school, but since his recent retirement he has kept mind and knife sharp by sharing his butchery skills with a new generation eager to get to know their food.

Richard first saws off the head, putting it to one side to boil up and make into brawn, before showing us how to separate the carcass into primal cuts, which we then divide into joints of meat. Our small class has a go, counting ribs before making careful insertions with a sharp knife, or swapping the knife for a serrated saw, pushing down slightly to cut through the bone. The loin gets divided into inch-thick tomahawk chops, peg bones poking out, or else set aside to be cured as bacon later. The shoulder is set to be roasted or slow cooked. The leg, salted and brined to become gammon and ham. Any offcuts from the butchery are thrown into a box at the end of the table, to be ground up into mince to make sausages later. And the belly joint? That's dinner for tonight, Roman style.

As hands on as the Marsh Pig has enabled me to get, the pig has already arrived dead, cleaned and ready to go; a trip to the abattoir is a step too far. This is true for most of us – even those who are prepared to handle the meat will draw the line at seeing an animal killed. It makes it easier to consume, if we don't see the creature before it arrives on our plate.

The Romans did not share this disconnection from their meat. Butchery, sacrifice and slaughter were a part of everyday life. Most citizens ate meat only rarely, but when they did it was typically from an animal they knew, that they had seen slaughtered, often as part of a ritual sacrifice for some holy day or festival.[2] Because of the value of an animal to a community, the occasion of its slaughter was a solemn one, a sacrifice not undertaken lightly – and a ritual held within full, deliberate view of the community.

Sacrifice means 'making sacred', and to acknowledge the solemnity and significance of the killing of an animal, it became bound up in holy ritual. The animal was named, patted and stroked as it was led towards the shrine, its neck and head hung with garlands of flowers and ribbons, anointed with perfumes. Water was poured on the creature's head, often causing it to nod or bow; the Romans took this to be an especially auspicious sign, as though the animal were consenting to its own death. The Romans had their own way of making peace with eating meat.

> Sacrifice means 'making sacred', and to acknowledge the solemnity and significance of the killing of an animal, it became bound up in holy ritual

The difficulties of preserving meat in a hot, Mediterranean climate meant that when an animal was slaughtered, the butchered meat had to be shared, or else wasted. The whole community gathered round not just to partake in the ritual of sacrifice, but also to enjoy the bounty.[3] Such events inevitably turned into feast days and festivals, and it is little wonder that in the West our own feast days remain associated with meats of various kinds: turkey and ham at Christmas, lamb at Easter, beef for Sunday lunch and barbecues on bank holidays. Just like the Romans, we still celebrate with an animal sacrifice.

Later that same evening, back in my own kitchen – wooden countertops and cluttered surfaces replacing the sterile steel and organised workspace from the morning – I follow suit. I turn the belly joint out on to the chopping board: the thick layer of pallid fat face down, meat blushing pink face up. I score the meat into squares, cutting deep enough to reach the fat, but not cutting all the way through.

I roll it up, tying it with twine and a butcher's knot, and place it into a dry, hot griddle pan to brown on all sides. Then, still sizzling, I move it to a roasting tin, and trussed up, into the oven it goes.

The clank of a roasting tray going into the oven reminds me of Sunday mornings when I was growing up, as breakfast dishes gave way to roast dinner preparations. While my mother was the reluctant weekday cook, for whom feeding our family of four was a chore, my father readily took over dinner duties on a Sunday. To him, provider of just the one meal a week, this was a joyful event, to be embraced with exuberance. Dad was an officer in the RAF, and he brought to the preparation of dinner the same sensibilities: timers and stopwatches, instructions and schedules pinned to the fridge, cooking as meticulously ordered as a military exercise.

While my mother was the reluctant weekday cook, for whom feeding our family of four was a chore, my father readily took over dinner duties on a Sunday

In this respect alone, I side with my dad. Alongside my trusty cookbook (Jamie Oliver for roast chicken, Nigella Lawson for roast potatoes, Delia for everything else), I double down on preparation when cooking a roast dinner, carefully working backwards from my intended serving time to plot out what needs to go on which oven shelf, and when.

Tonight's dinner inevitably feeds into my research. I'm using an ancient Roman recipe from the world's oldest surviving cookbook, *De Re Coquinaria*, known more commonly as 'Apicius', after the first century Roman chef thought to have authored it. Apicius and I swiftly clash, for he lists neither cooking times, nor quantities, so I'm left to my own devices. Rather than reach for my phone to look up comparable recipes, I pause a moment and draw upon my own experiences. I want the pork to char ever so slightly, the fatty layer to begin to melt: 45 minutes at 190C.

When the pork re-emerges from the oven, it has become something else. The skin, close to but not quite burnt, is crisp and golden, the juicy flesh just starting to brown. I cut the twine with a pair of kitchen scissors and watch as the joint slowly unfurls, returning to its original shape. The meat is just about cooked through, ready for its final transformation.

While it rests, I grind peppercorns, celery seeds, ginger and cumin together in a shallow mortar, adding them to a large pan along with a heavy dash of fish sauce and a few glugs of sweet red dessert wine. The smell is spicy, fragrant, but also ever so slightly rancid – the fish sauce, threatening to overwhelm as it always does. The Romans – who added it to everything, sweet and savoury alike, and were even known to drink it diluted with water – must have been immune to its pungency. I remain wary not to drown out every other flavour, but as soon as the pan is placed over a low heat the kitchen instantly stinks of rotting fish. My partner Ben, sceptical of the whole endeavour, has been watching from the doorway. He responds to my culinary practice with a scowl, turning the extractor fan to high, flinging open a window and withdrawing to the living room to wait for me to finish.

Just as the sauce begins to bubble, I take up a knife and the rested pork. Moving quickly, I slice the blade sideways through the meat, between the fat and the crackling, sending the ofellae – highly-

Spooning the pork and sauce into our bowls, I consider the metamorphosis... from whole carcass this morning to cubes of spiced, roasted pork tonight

seasoned meat pieces – tumbling into the pan one after the other. Then they are stirred into the sauce, the heat is turned up, and it all cooks down.[4]

Spooning the pork and sauce into our bowls, I consider the metamorphosis that has taken place, from whole carcass this morning to cubes of spiced, roasted pork tonight. Once-proud pig, king of his farmyard, cut down to tiny morsels. The pork, wondrously burnt around the edges, is kept juicy by the fatty layer. The sauce has transformed too. The fishiness has disappeared, replaced by a hint of citrus and an intense, earthy savouriness that only adds to the pork's succulence.[5]

Ben sniffs the pork suspiciously. 'Did you put fish sauce in this?'

I nod. He sniffs again, but then to my surprise, takes a bite of pork. And then another. I smile to myself.

'What?' Ben asks.

'Oh, nothing.' I say, wondering whether Apicius' wife had the same reaction to his cooking. H

1 Translation taken from Grainger and Grocock. *Apicius: A Critical Edition with an Introduction and English Translation*. Prospect Books (2006)

2 Visser, Margaret. *The Rituals of Dinner*. Penguin Random House (2017), p35

3 Ibid., p33

4 Grainger, Sally. *Cooking Apicius*. Prospect Books (2006), p77

5 Segnit, Niki. *The Flavour Thesaurus*. Bloomsbury (2010), p161

Recipes from my Father

by Sue Hann

1. Peanut butter on toast

Ingredients: *Panda 'American Style' Peanut Butter, Brennans white sliced bread.*

Method: *Set toaster to high. Burn one slice of white bread. Spread straight away with peanut butter. Eat, in silence, standing up.*

It was always Brennans Bread that we had at home, the white sliced pan loaf that came in a yellow waxed paper packet with their slogan 'Today's Bread Today' in red script. It was soft and pillowy in the centre, with a rounded brown crust. It was so soft that the act of buttering would tear holes in the bread. My father got around this by toasting each slice hard, burning it so that the crusts were black, the centre a dark brown. I can only imagine that he must have liked it that way, enjoyed the acrid taste of char. He spread it with Panda peanut butter, which contained added sugar and all kinds of nasties; the brand was popular in the eighties before clean eating was a thing. My father ate this single slice standing at the sink, staring out at the back garden, with a mug of sweet tea that he slurped in long gulps. My mother would complain about this if she was within earshot.

If my father offered me this breakfast, already made and waiting on a side plate, I would study the quality of his silence, try to gauge his mood. If I judged it safe, I might dare to tell him that it was a little burnt for me. He would scrape the worst of the black from the underside of the toast into the sink, before returning it, wordlessly, to my plate.

2. Chicken Soy Sauce

Ingredients (an incomplete list): *Chicken stock (from a cube), Root ginger, chopped, Dark soy sauce, Hard boiled eggs, Chicken on the bone*

My father's speciality was chicken soy sauce which he cooked in a big metal pot on the hob: chicken on the bone with hard-boiled eggs floating in a thin gravy of dark soy sauce. Not that he cooked very often, but if he did, it would always be this dish. I never saw my father consult a recipe book and, thinking about it now, I wonder if this was a meal that his parents had made for him, something that recalled his childhood 10,000 kilometres away in Malaysia. He didn't prepare it for particular occasions, or at predictable intervals, so I wonder if the dish was something that my father cooked when homesick, longing for something other than the bland 'meat and two veg' diet of eighties Ireland. He never said. But then he didn't say much in general. I'd like to say that this recipe was something that he handed down to me, but he never showed us how to make his chicken soy sauce. We probably never showed any interest. It's too late to ask, now that he is separated from my mother and took that opportunity to separate himself from his children while he was at it. I think about things my father left behind, try to think about things he gave me; though the list is so much shorter than the things he withheld.

Now, as an adult, I have a craving for this rich and salty chicken dish, and I try to work out how he made it, thinking that perhaps I can recreate it. Thinking also that perhaps this is something of his that I can hold on to, in the absence of anything else.

Method:
1. First chop the chicken into large pieces.
My father had a meat cleaver, kept in the second drawer, for cutting through the carcass. We had to be careful, us children, putting hands into the knife drawer. I don't remember seeing him joint the chicken for this dish. What I do remember is the sound of the cleaver being brought down from a height, the crunch of bone, the thwack of the blade, and then the moment of silence, the slight pause as my father pulled the blade of the cleaver free from the groove it made in the wooden board. The noise reverberated against the kitchen counter, the cleaver dropping like a guillotine again and again until the chicken was transformed from a carcass to a pile of bony chunks.

2. Make the gravy base
Use fresh ginger and other aromatics (you'll have to guess at this: perhaps star anise?) to flavour a poaching broth of dark soy sauce. Don't stint on the ginger. Add the chicken pieces to the poaching liquid in a deep saucepan.

My father was a big believer in ginger. He sliced it, peel on, with the cleaver, then turned the blade on its side, pushing the sliced root onto its flat surface before sliding it into the pot. His hands, small and fine-boned like his frame, were surprisingly competent while cooking, as at home with a blade as with his accountant's pencil.

> ## His hands, small and fine boned like his frame, were surprisingly competent while cooking, as at home with a blade as with his accountant's pencil

'You'll never catch a cold if you eat ginger every day' he'd say as he stirred the pot with the wooden spoon. And he was a good advert for his own advice, very rarely sick. In my father's eyes, catching a cold was something that you brought on yourself. If I went outside to play without a coat, my father would erupt into a roar, his words as sudden and as lethal as sniper fire.

'If you get sick, I'll throw you into hospital and leave you there.'

I made sure I ate the slices of ginger, the fire they left in my mouth preferable to this threat of abandonment.

3. Hard boil the eggs
Add the eggs to the saucepan and allow them to hard boil in the broth. My father lowered them into the liquid on a metal serving spoon, one by one, so the shells wouldn't crack. He could be careful with some things.

As a child, I didn't like the grey rim around the yolk, caused by a reaction of sulphur from the egg white and iron from the egg yolk, but I ate it nonetheless, brought up to finish my plate no matter what.

4. Serve with steamed rice, no sides.
My father would make the rice in the green electric
rice cooker. He bought the jasmine rice in a large
woven sack from Asia Market, loading it into the
boot of the car with jars of soy sauce, packets of
dehydrated noodles, and all the other food that
wasn't available in the supermarket in Ireland back
then. The hessian sack lived in a corner of the utility
room, and I liked to dip my hand in there and feel
the grains, hard and cool against my fingers. There
were no vegetables in the dish or as a side. My
father didn't go in for fripperies like greens.

There were no vegetables in the dish or as a side. My father didn't go in for fripperies like greens

The chicken was tender, falling off the bone, and
made even tastier by its rare appearance on the
dinner table. It lasted a couple of days, the chicken
soy sauce, the broth assuming a deeper, richer
flavour with time. We ate it sitting on high wooden
stools at the kitchen counter, my brother and I
sitting opposite our two parents like chess players.
My father ate in his customary silence, eyes down,
hunched over his plate.

3. Prawn Crackers
Ingredients: *Dehydrated prawn crackers, sunflower oil.*
Method: *Heat oil in deep-fat fryer. Insert crackers into very
hot oil. Remove after a few seconds. Drain on kitchen paper.
Serve immediately.*

Occasionally, during the summer holidays, if my father was in a good mood, he might make prawn crackers. Not the cheap and nasty white things that came with Chinese takeaways, which looked and tasted like Styrofoam, but the proper flesh-coloured ones that actually tasted of prawn. My mother made him cook them outside because she didn't like the smell they left in the kitchen. My father took the deep fat fryer out to the side passage, running an extension lead from the kitchen out the back door. That he was going to this much trouble for a snack was a definite sign that he was feeling jolly, a relatively rare occurrence.

Sensing these good vibrations, I would hover, like a bee to a prized nectar, watching as he squatted down on his haunches, in his rubber flip-flops that he called 'slippers', dropping the dehydrated prawn discs into the wire basket and lowering them into the bubbling oil. A noisy crackle and hiss as they hit the fat.

'Stand back, it'll spatter' my father would warn, and I would, retreating to the safety of the patch of grass in the back garden. When they were done, my father scooped the crackers out, shook them firmly, and left them to drain on kitchen paper. If left out too long, they'd become chewy and plastic-tasting.

'Quick, come, eat' he'd say.

I would run, hands outstretched, eager to take anything he had to give. **H**

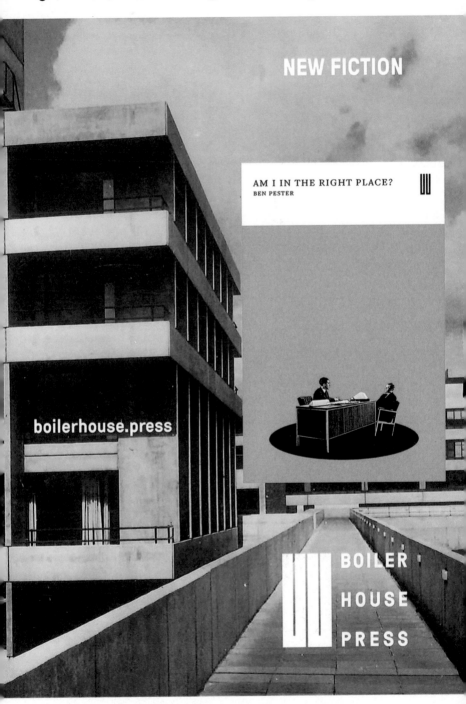

"A glorious, shimmering and strange collection."

NEW FICTION

AM I IN THE RIGHT PLACE?
BEN PESTER

boilerhouse.press

BOILER
HOUSE
PRESS

– Irenosen Okojie, author of *Nudibranch*

by Noah Birksted-Breen

(St. Petersburg, 1997)
Snow

The front door is rough to the touch: blood-red metal. I drunkenly pull the key from my pocket. After a couple of attempts, I manage to insert it in the lock. There's a click, but the door doesn't open. I yank the black handle.

I remember the bar on the inside. My landlady, Gulya, must have pulled it down. It's a solid metal safety bar, attached from the inside wall to the front door. There's no way I can get in. She would have to release it. Every apartment has one of these – the feature dates from the various phobias of the Soviet era. It is important for Russians to know that nobody can enter without their consent. If intruders want to force their way in, they'll have to wrench off a chunk of wall. Of course, it only works against burglary. State security can get you lots of other ways. Some Soviet dissidents used to sit outside their front door with a packed suitcase all night long, for weeks on end, when they knew arrest was imminent. They didn't want their families to bear witness. Better to walk off voluntarily with the secret police. Now it's a different time.

A time of gangster capitalism. Rumours abound of business 'take-overs' where the new company boss removes the previous owner with a bullet to the head; a headless corpse later discovered on a road leading out of town. So, Russians continue to use their security bars into the 'democracy' being constructed in the 1990s.

I try to decide what to do next, but can't think straight. I'm feeling nauseous.

———

We're dancing to Western pop. My university friend, Dario, and I feel hopeful that we might be exuding a sexy foreign aura. We don't conform to dominant Russian trends. Six years after communism has ended, Russian clothes, haircuts and glasses nostalgically evoke the 1970s. In fact, they look so convincingly like the genuine articles, they probably are. We're two university students on a year abroad, trying our luck, in a bunker which has been repurposed for nightlife, at the outskirts of the city.

It's fun until about 2am, but now I'm bored. I wish we could leave. Unfortunately, we need a metro to get back to the city and it doesn't re-start for another three hours. So I do my best to keep dancing with our Russian dates, who seem to have endless energy. My date, Valya, is sensible and funny. She's a bright literature student from working class parents. I get drunk enough to ask her if she'll record some poetry on a cassette for me.

A couple of hours later, I suggest we go and wait by the entrance to the metro in case it opens early, so we stand by the metal grille and for the best part of an hour we stomp in the snow. By now, I'm unable to talk from exhaustion. The three of them keep joking, mainly about how angry I look.

As the metro pulls into the city, Valya asks me:

'Do you want to come back with me? I live with my parents. You can sleep on a fold-out bed.'

My Russian has improved by late October, almost two months into my year abroad, but it still only caters for binary choices

It seems too confusing, so I say, *nyet*. My Russian has improved by late October, almost two months into my year abroad, but it still only caters for binary choices. After a few stops, we part ways, going *po domam*: each to their own home. Later I regret it, but this foreign country isn't turning me into an extrovert. I've brought an innate anxiety of human contact with me.

I exit the metro and walk through the park. The rancid smell of food waste suddenly hits me, emanating from an overflowing pile of rubbish on the pavement. Waste collection isn't fully functional in this city. The pile sits by the gated entrance to an internal courtyard behind a residential building. Briefly, I wonder if I can cut through the courtyard to the other side, the way many locals do – but I don't know the shortcuts well enough.

I enter the pistachio-green apartment block on the corner of Tatarskii Lane. As I walk up the wide concrete stairs, running my palm along the handrail, I recall my mother's parting advice: 'Never accept cheap Russian champagne from strangers. It might be spiked and you'll end up in a coma.' At the club I only drank beer that I'd paid for myself. Her warning lingers in my mind longer than the compulsory HIV/AIDS blood test that I had to get from a private UK clinic in order to obtain a Russian visa.

I ring the doorbell again, just in case. Gulya's in her sixties, though she looks twenty years older than that. She's a five-foot, slender woman with wiry black hair. Her face is wrinkly and intelligent, she has lively eyes and a feminine, gravelly voice. She shuffles slowly along the wooden floors of her apartment and spends a lot of time watching television. It's a quiet retirement for a former geologist who travelled across the Soviet Union during communism, surveying the country's landscape and natural resources. The TV is always turned up loud. Her hearing isn't good. I wonder – can I wake her by ringing the doorbell in increasingly long and insistent bursts? It's 6.20am and my bladder is full. I wonder what a Russian student would do: would he shout and scream until she came to the door? I look woefully at my fist, pressed against the door; it drops to my side. Silenced by a sense of decorum, I sit down heavily on the worn grey step.

There's a large white radiator, half a flight down. The communal stairwell is dusty, poorly maintained. The radiator's too hot for me to sit on with my full weight; so I perch, trying to prop my elbow on my leg and cupping my hand for a pillow. Surely she'll wake up soon? I decide to ring the bell every half hour.

—

Dobro pozhalovat'! Welcome to Mother Russia. As I step onto the bus outside the airport in the last week of August, the driver, who has a cigarette dangling between his lips, looks at me angrily. I'm holding out my fare for the ticket, but – much to his annoyance – I've offered to pay with a 100-rouble note (about two pounds). He shrugs at me. He's not willing to give me change. I'm new to this, so naively I refuse to budge. Passengers start shouting at me: *Molodoi chelovek!* Young man! *Doesn't this idiot know how things are done in this country?* They're in a hurry and I'm delaying them. From my neat colourful clothes, which reek of Western optimism, as well as my poor Russian accent, they understand at a glance that I'm not one of them. I ignore the shouting, mainly because I'm not sure – is it me they're shouting at? What did I do wrong? I've come equipped with a worldview imbued with the firm belief that the customer is always right. After a few minutes he decides I'm too much trouble and reaches over to get me 80 roubles, shaking his head in disbelief. I glance up at the picture card hanging on his mirror: a naked, large-breasted woman kneeling on a beach. The objects on the dashboard – a tabloid newspaper, a well-thumbed paperback and a fluffy kid's toy – suggests he's the only person who drives this bus.

As we reach our first, then second, then third stop, I look out of the grubby windows at the bright, midday light. The man behind me suddenly asks: 'Are you getting off?'

His words are slurred and I smell vodka on his breath. I've learnt about this custom in preparation for my year in Russia: not the drinking, but the special method of exiting a bus or train, by asking people around you, in advance – although I'm also braced for the drinking.

> Passengers start shouting at me: *Molodoi chelovek! Young man! Doesn't this idiot know how things are done in this country?*

'No,' I reply; and we do a slow shuffle dance around each other so that he can move nearer to the exit, and I can edge my way further in.

There aren't enough handrails. I'm in the middle of the crowded bus and I can't reach any of them. The road is bumpy. People are leaning against my back, apparently unconcerned that our bodies are touching. If the driver needs to brake suddenly, I'll have no choice but to fall onto my fellow passengers.

—

My elbow slips off my knee. It's almost 7am and I've had a few minutes of fitful sleep. Now I've had a brilliant idea. I can use some coins in my pocket to call Gulya from a payphone. Surely the ringing will wake her? I need to keep enough roubles to buy a *bublik*, a tasteless bagel that I often eat at lunchtime between lectures at the State University. The bakery on the corner will open at 8am. My change will be enough for one call.

I slot money into the phone box, shivering, and listen to the sound of ringing. There's no limit to how long you can let a phone ring if nobody answers it, and even though it's minus five degrees Celsius, I resolve to stand here for as long as it takes.

—

After one week in Russia, it's time to phone home. I don't want to use my host's phone as she's living off a basic state pension. On Sunday, I go to the Post Office and pay upfront for half an hour's conversation. The woman at the counter seems angry with me. I've already encountered a couple of angry shopkeepers and I'm starting to wonder if this is the default mode for customer service in Russia. She tells me to pick up the receiver in booth number 3 and wait for her command.

At first there's nothing and then suddenly she barks through the receiver: 'England: speak now! Speak, England!'

After hearing my mother's distant and tinny voice on the patchy international line, I walk back to the metro, agitated; unsatisfied.

The escalator carrying me down into the belly of the metro is two or three times longer than those on the London Underground. Friends turn to each other from their respective steps and conduct involved conversations on their way down. One man and woman hold each other in a tender hug, eyes closed, oblivious to the *up* onlookers.

At first there's nothing and then suddenly she barks through the receiver: 'England: speak now! Speak, England!'

I hear shouting. There's a woman at the bottom, waving her arms. I angle my camera to take a photo of the metro's fake chandeliers. As I arrive at the concourse, I realise she's shouting at me, although I only catch the words *fotoapparat*, camera, and *nelzya*, not allowed, and I nod furiously. She lets me go, and she steps back into the privacy of her booth, positioned between the *up* and the *down* escalators.

Wanting to escape the scene of my dressing down, I resolve to get onto the first train that arrives at the nearest platform, and then work out if I'm going the right way.

—

Universities start at the end of August in Russia. It's my first day in a foreign country: I hope I won't get lost on the twenty-minute walk from Gulya's apartment. Before crossing one of the many canals in Piter, as locals affectionately call their city, I approach a palatial yellow building. There are a few limousines with black-tinted windows parked outside. Two men exit the building and I slow my pace. They're dressed identically to each other:

black suits, dark sunglasses and each man has a peroxide blonde on display by his side. I'm excited to be seeing my first New Russians, the nobodies who bought up whole companies and industries at the end of communism, and then kept on buying new assets during the mass privatisations of the mid-1990s.

I'm excited to be seeing my first New Russians, the nobodies who bought up whole companies and industries at the end of communism

They linger on the steps, chatting; I cross the road. Now danger takes on a different form. The rules governing roads offer a display of brutal honesty – consistent with the dominant social conventions of the time: whoever is strongest has the right of way. Within a week of arriving, I understand that if you approach a pedestrian crossing at the same time as a speeding car, you let the car go.

—

In late September, there are a few balmy weeks: a *bab'e leto*, an old woman's summer. I'm still feeling adrift in this city and I visit one of the largest Russian Orthodox Churches. I hope that seeing a top-ten tourist site will boost my morale. The vaulted ceiling is impressive and there's a smell of incense. The guidebook informs me that a chorus of male-only voices will emanate from behind the pulpit – invisible to the congregation. Evidently, the Orthodox religious experience is intended to be mystical. And also uncomfortable: there are no pews, only a single hard wooden bench near a stone column for the elderly or disabled.

Near me, a woman with a scarf wrapped neatly around her head is talking quietly to an icon in a hushed and intimate tone. I wonder which saint is her special one: the one her parents chose for her at birth, which she'll celebrate on her saint's day each year.

I glance over to the far side of the church. The daylight is slanting through a tall, narrow window. I notice a man waving his arms in a panic as if fighting off a wasp. He's standing inside the ledge of the window, framed by bright light. I feel awed by his hand-waving display, as he swooshes his arms up and down. I feel a strange *toska*, a sadness I can't explain, a nostalgia for something I've never experienced. I stand and watch the man – until I realise he's cleaning the windows. Even then, I choose to stand and watch him for twenty minutes, which is longer than the woman confiding in her saint. For the first time, I wonder how this year in Russia will change me.

———

'*Tovarishchi!* Comrades! President Yeltsin has appointed a new Prime Minister!'

My Russian improves when I watch TV news, so I watch a lot. A few weeks in the country has given me an appetite to learn faster. It's Sunday and I'm watching with Gulya. I can't think of anything to ask her, I'm nineteen and painfully shy, and she's already aware of how limited my Russian is. So we sit silently in front of a live broadcast. The new PM is chairing a cabinet meeting. He turns to a member of his cabinet and asks: *Kakie u Vas obyazannosti?* What do you do?

At first, I wonder – how can a Prime Minister be so ignorant? Then I change my mind. It takes guts to be that honest in front of the entire Russian public. Still, it's quite funny that the PM has to ask each cabinet member to explain their role. The minister looks astounded and states in a loud expressionless voice: 'I'm in charge of finance'.

The PM continues: 'So does economics fall within your remit?'

This feels even worse than Yeltsin's recent gaffe, when he showed up totally pissed in front of the international press. The finance minister begins to mumble a reply but the PM cuts him off:

'You *are* responsible for economics! You must meet the targets set by President!' The minister looks sheepish now, so the PM continues: 'There is no excuse for failure!'

Now I understand. It was all a ruse to show who is in charge. The finance minister stares down at the table in front of him like a nine-year old.

The PM turns to his next cabinet member.

——

By 8.20am, I've finished my *bublik* and I'm feeling relieved, having also emptied my bladder behind a skip in the inner courtyard of Gulya's building.

I accept that there's no hope of sleeping in my bed today, when I'm finally let in. I'll ask Gulya if she's making *grechka*, buckwheat porridge, and can I please have some?

This feels even worse than Yeltsin's recent gaffe, when he showed up totally pissed in front of the international press

A few minutes later, I'm already starting to sober up. Evidently, I have no deep connection to Russian conventions, at least the ones around drinking.

—

One evening in late November, after Gulya's gone to make herself a tea, I'm flicking through the channels when I come across the Army Channel. The TV distracts me from thinking too much. Two months of lectures in Russian has improved my pronunciation. I know how to contort my face into an exaggerated smile, or pout while speaking, to make the murkiest sounds: y (ы) – a guttural vowel from the back of the throat like a staccato cry, and zh (ж) – a buzzing complaint of a consonant. I've learnt strange new words, which become neutered and cerebral when translated, like *obruset*: to *become* Russian. I'll be on a plane to England in a month. I'm due to return to St. Petersburg in the new year but I wonder if I shouldn't just go to France instead, my other undergraduate language?

When Gulya comes back out and sits on the sofa next to me, I realise this may be my last proper chance to talk to her. We chat briefly about our respective days, then sit in silence.

A soldier speaks to the grave of his fallen captain: it's a grainy Soviet spy thriller. The camera pans back to two men in a Lada, eavesdropping. They're holding an extremely old-fashioned listening device, longer than a telescope. Can they really hear the soldier divulging his crimes in the cemetery? The soldier bids farewell to his captain. The secret police are revving their engine. Will they do a hit and run? They decide on a 'neutral solution', driving off to their next job.

There are two words for drunk in Russian, *pianyi* and *zapoi*. The latter implies a type of drunkenness which is more profound and enduring

Next, there's a programme with the latest Army news, introduced by the Minister of Regional Development; I hear Gulya tutting under her breath. He praises a new MiG helicopter design as a paradigm of socio-political achievement. I catch myself staring with fascination at the dazzling technology on display. I ask if we can switch channels.

———

Within a couple of weeks of arriving, we've found a workable system: my mother calls at an agreed time on the landline – it won't cost Gulya anything. I'm in my room; Gulya suddenly calls me to the phone. Frowning, I walk into the living room – it's not our agreed time. My mother tells me: 'I heard something

on the radio. A nuclear explosion near St. Petersburg.
I didn't catch the details. Get ready to leave
immediately. I'll find out more, wait by the phone!'

So I wait. And wait. And when she calls back
ninety minutes later, my mother says she may have
got it wrong, but – 'be ready to leave at short notice'.

No further information ever emerges. I wonder
if that's how her grandparents felt when they fled
Eastern Europe in 1908 to avoid the pogroms.

———

I'm involved in a drama club in the UK, so perhaps
theatre can make me feel more at home? Through
October, I call Russian venues. Finally, I reach N——
on the number in the phone book, and ask if I can
meet him at his studio theatre.

'Sure,' he replies, 'but I'm not available right
now, I'm on a *zapoi*'.

There are two words for drunk in Russian, *pianyi* and
zapoi. The latter implies a type of drunkenness which
is more profound and enduring. A transformative
state of being, lasting three days or more.

Five days later I meet N—— . In the UK, it is the
norm for theatre-makers to say that they *love everything*
even when they don't, but in Russia, it's crucial to
hate somebody and to say so. N—— spends half an hour
telling me how much he hates the new production
by K——. Finally, he asks me to say something about
myself. He asks: 'Which theatre do you hate?'

That evening I attend a production at N——'s
theatre, followed by a post-show discussion. There, I

discover that – because it's happening in public – it's vital not only to say that you hate a production but to shout about it.

—

I employ my love of theatre to create an amateur production with other British students at the university. It's early in the morning. We are blurry-eyed, but ready to work. A security guard lets us in. We wander onto the stage knowing what lies ahead. We have to build the set, get the lights rigged and then do our first show later that day, as part of a festival organised by N——. As we look out into the auditorium, we become aware of a technical problem. This production, designed for a studio theatre of sixty seats, is now going to play at an eight hundred-seater. I smile wryly: 'We may have to make a few changes.'

I hope that the audience will put it down to foreign eccentricity.

A man appears. He has his own little area at the side of the stage. He looks fantastically cheerful, and wishes us a good morning. As we build the set, he runs around sweeping the whole floor. He sweeps back and forth, around us, under our feet which we raise obligingly, and then he sweeps every item of the set which we put on stage: the cupboard, the carpets, the bed. I try to stop him – not out of any moral rectitude. 'The set represents a run-down flat,' I explain, 'so any dust is good for us. It helps to show that the main character lives in disarray.'

He smiles at me knowingly.

'Ah, yes,' he says, 'I see. But anyway, dust is dust.' He resumes dusting with a reinvigorated passion.

This man is a sort of 'best of Russia'. He has a job to do and he'll do it. In a country that can get to minus 60 degrees in the winter, and which is blighted by corruption, this *stage-genie*, as I come to think of him, is what keeps the country going. His bloody-mindedness can be frustrating. You can try to reason with him, cajole and flatter him, you can tease him and maybe even scream at him to change his ways, but the stage-genie will not waver. Actors will come and go, theatre managements will come and go, but this man will be here, holding up Russia on his shoulders, dusting and cleaning Russia through good times and bad.

He resumes dusting with a reinvigorated passion. This man is a sort of 'best of Russia'. He has a job to do and he'll do it

After half an hour, we become acutely aware that something is missing. Namely, two technicians whose job is to set up the lighting for our show. They've promised to be here when we arrive. I tap my feet: 'They'll be here any minute'.

We busy ourselves with props. Ten minutes later, I call the curator of the festival. 'I'm sorry,' I start politely, 'but the lighting technicians aren't here. We did come at the right time, didn't we?'

She frets and calls the technicians. 'They're on their way. Ten minutes.'

Things are going to be delayed.

Twenty minutes later – still no sign.

'OK,' she says sheepishly in a voice which indicates that she'll do anything for me if it's within her power, 'one of them is on his way, the other isn't answering his phone.'

I feel the blood draining from my face. 'Sorry, what do you mean on his way? And what do you mean *not answering his phone?*'

The curator is from N—'s studio theatre, which is run as a private venture. It has a team of fifty people, who aren't paid much but are deeply committed to their art. She tries to explain: 'If your performance was going to run on our stage, we'd all be there right now... but the large state theatres produce low-quality commercial work, so you see... the staff don't always feel they have to turn up.'

I feel the blood draining from my face. 'Sorry, what do you mean on his way? And what do you mean *not answering his phone?*

I know I should be furious, I know I should shout and scream. That's what a Russian director would do, and that's why their lighting technicians would turn up on time. But instead I clamber up the stairs to the empty technicians' box and look down at the vast auditorium with its plush seating. Resignation is also a survival skill in Russia. I glance down at the stage-genie who is happily singing to himself and reading a book in his little hideaway.

When the first lighting technician turns up three hours late, he mumbles an apology so quietly under his breath that he might as well have said:

I hate theatre. Fortunately, he then runs around doing everything we ask of him – his metre-long blond hair bouncing around doesn't impede him, nor does his gloomy face: this man is truly fast. Amazingly, we start to get back on schedule. We perform our little show later that day, a contemporary Russian play by Oleg Bogaev, to polite applause. We don't hold a post-show discussion.

Everything sounds echoey. My feet crunch down on the hard snow as I walk over to the main road near Tatarskii Lane. There's a tiny yellow sign, hanging two-thirds of the way up the lamppost. It's a tram-stop. There's no way of knowing which tram numbers correspond with which destinations, you just have to know. This country is run by word-of-mouth. Fortunately, it's mid-December and by now I know which tram I need. It's 11pm; trams at this time are unreliable. I listen attentively to the crunching of snow under my feet as I pace backwards and forwards to stay warm. The sound is muted and the clouds hang low. There's a sense of un-realness, and I wonder if I've missed the last tram of the night.

Snowflakes flutter capriciously – sometimes they dance wildly around before starting their descent downwards, while other flakes dance upwards before swirling off sideways. The streetlamp throws a strange yellow hue onto the parked cars, turning them into silhouettes. I pull the flaps of my winter hat closer to my ears, tug my scarf over my mouth and try not to focus on the biting cold which is freezing my fingers through my gloves. Everything in this city was built to impress. Stone houses, the size of palaces, lean menacingly over pedestrians. Over the course of twenty minutes, six or seven people appear at the same lamppost, also hoping for a final tram. They stand stoically, faces buried into their fur coats. One middle-aged woman stands proud, not even attempting to hide her face against the cold. I imitate her, assuming a rocky facial expression and angry eyes. But I'm not made for this. My back hunches over into a shivering bundle as I wonder *how* and *what* and *why*; my face softens and tears run down my cheeks with cold and confusion, as I whisper to myself – *why am I here?* My feet are frozen now as I've stopped walking and my winter boots are sinking into a heap of snow. I become aware that my frozen toes aren't really part of me anymore.

Marking time more energetically, the snow lands faster on my face. It's minus twenty degrees Celsius, but the gusty wind makes it feel ten degrees colder again. When I see the tram in the distance, running along its tracks, I imagine seeing it from above – a tram connecting my room at Gulya's apartment to Valya's parents' flat: a bright journey cutting through the impossible winter night like a fairground ride. But the strangeness of living in a foreign city, the unrootedness of it, is dizzyingly sharper and denser with a relationship that started in late November when snow was already falling thickly.

—

Valya calls suddenly at 10.50pm a few days before Christmas – which doesn't surprise me anymore. Phone calls were free during communism and, without any other luxuries or entertainments, Russians who were bored and/or sleepless with anxiety got into the habit of phoning each other at any hour. She invites me to spend the night in her parents' single-room flat.

As we drift off to sleep, I wonder whether our relationship will last through my two weeks in England over Christmas

There's a bookcase dividing the living room, so Valya's mum and stepdad can sleep on the fold-out sofa on one side, while we're on the other; she's on a single bed and I have a fold-out camp-bed. We'll hear her parents snoring tonight, and we'll whisper to each other about the places we want to travel in Russia: villages that don't connect to roads in Yakutia; wild forests where no person has ever set foot in Kamchatka.

We don't dare have sex, not at night. If her parents go out in the day, we'll ask them where they're going. Then we'll shut the door behind them, waiting a sensible amount of time before undressing, and to be totally safe, we'll pull down the bar across the door.

As we drift off to sleep, I wonder whether our relationship will last through my two weeks in England over Christmas. I haven't confided in Valya that I'm unsure whether to come back.

I doze against the front door, it's past 9am and my mind is empty. An old man is coming up the stairs. He doesn't seem to notice me. There are three levels of friends in Russia – *znakomye*, acquaintances; *priyateli*, friends; and *druziya*, friends. You don't *islit dusha*, pour out your soul, with the first and second categories. That's what *druziya* are for. But to this stony-faced man walking past me, I'm *nikto*. Nobody.

I hear a thudding noise inside the apartment and I jump up from the grey step. I bang my fist on the door. I wait. I bang again.

It must have been the cat. Or perhaps I imagined it. Is this a nightmare? Perhaps this is like the Russian short story I read recently about a man who shrinks… His wife is angry at him, but there's nothing he can do, he gets smaller and smaller, until he simply disappears.

———

I wave my arm into the road and wait for a car to stop. Flights are cheaper because it's Christmas Day. The Soviets demoted Christmas for being too religious. New Year became the big deal. Anyway it's a normal working day for many Russians. A smart black car pulls over to the curb and the driver rolls down his window.

'Airport', I say, '1000 roubles.'

He looks skeptical and I wait for the haggling to begin. But he nods, a cigarette dangling between his lips, and we're off.

The city looks beautiful in the snow. All the rubbish and nasty smells are buried under its white brilliance. We speed along the Neva River past the Hermitage. I breathe in his cigarette smoke, too polite to complain, and enjoy watching the stone buildings race past. Soon we'll have to drive through the grim high-rise suburbs. His curiosity gets the better of him.

'Are you Polish?'

I glow with pride at his mistake.

'Estonian?'

I explain myself – a Londoner who fell under the spell of Russian novels, their passion and angst. He laughs but says nothing. It's the usual reason foreigners come to his country. He seems to change his mind about me, and asks if I like his birth city.

'*Nalyubilsya.*' I've fallen in love. Wrong grammar but he gets the idea and laughs.

> **He seems to change his mind about me, and asks if I like his birth city. '*Nalyubilsya.*' I've fallen in love**

We chat about politics, like old friends. And religion. And literature – Agatha Christie and Dostoevsky. We are now driving through the seemingly endless forest outside the city. As a child, his mother told him what she really thought of the Soviet leaders, the taps splashing noisily into the sink while she whispered her truths.

He got a good education and became a chauffeur for a Soviet diplomat – so things were good for him, he had access to special shops. I'm greedy to hear more. He suddenly recites a poem – reams of verse about a poet in the Soviet times who returns from exile to find his old friends missing, disappeared. He lives on a darkened step, aching with love for his city. I catch certain phrases: the stabbing beauty of spectral streets; ghostly voices in his friends' empty apartments.

As we pull up to the airport, the man grins and hands me a piece of paper, on which he's scribbled his name and home phone number.

'Call me anytime.'

—

Around 10.15am, I hear loud noises in the apartment: a bowl banging on the kitchen counter, a metal pan clanging onto the gas stove. When I ring the bell, the apartment goes silent. I curse my decision to go clubbing all over again. Then suddenly, there's creaking – metal scraping metal. Gulya lifts the bar and swings open the front door. She sees me, and without looking particularly surprised, she says: 'Oh, good morning!'

I shout angrily that I want to live in a country where everybody is honest and passionate

I nod at her and walk silently past, into the hallway. I glance into the kitchen to my right and see the tomcat sitting in the *fortochka*, the little opening at the top of the window; he likes to perch there, half in and half out. I turn back and mutter *dobroe utro* to her, good morning. Then I step into my room and shut the door behind me. I lie down on my bed, falling asleep within seconds. I have a vivid dream about being back in England, in which I hate my family and everybody else, and I shout angrily that I want to live in a country where everybody is honest and passionate.

'Why don't you move to Russia then?' my mum asks, although she's crying, clearly hoping I won't. **H**

"The lecturers were excellent, the MA provided great opportunities for working on external projects and meeting students from as far away as the Bolivian Andes. Most importantly, I am now a markedly better writer and well on my way to a literary career."

Joe, Creative Non-fiction MA Student

**Manchester
Metropolitan
University**

**The Manchester
Writing School**

Study Creative Non-Fiction

at the UK's longest running online MA/MFA programme with the Manchester Writing School at Manchester Met

- Join one of the country's largest postgraduate creative writing communities.

- Study from home with an international cohort of students via online distance learning.

- Develop your writing skills through a blend of practical and peer review workshops led by award-winning writers.

- Explore the range of sub-genres in this popular field: Autobiography, Green Writing, Literary Journalism, Nature Writing, Quest Biography, Place Writing, Memoir, Long Form Essay, Travel Writing and Historical Non-fiction.

- Examine a diverse range of twentieth and twenty-first century creative non-fiction texts with leading critical academics.

- Professional development opportunities with industry experts, and bonus sessions with published creative non-fiction authors from around the world.

Apply by end of August to guarantee a September 2021 start and by end of November for January 2022.

mmu.ac.uk/english/creative-writing

The Pen: A Collection

by Sally Gander

1.

Your favourite pen is a Pilot G-2 07. Always blue.
It has a comfortable rubberized grip, a click
mechanism so that there is no lid to lose, and
the ink gives fluidity to your thoughts as it glides
across the page. It has taken thirty years to unbind
your writing self, each word moving towards this
expansive state of being. Belief is everything.

2.

Back when you are a novice writer, you believe
that marriage and children are a pre-destined
path. Your sisters do these things before you, and
so you follow, you and your new husband signing
the marriage certificate in a small room at the back
of the church. You don't remember the pen you
used, but you imagine it was an elegant fountain
pen, the ink symbolic of hope flowing into your
future lives together. The use of signatures to bind
agreements began with The Statute of Frauds Act
in 1677. It follows that men of government decided
that marriage should also be sealed with ink on
the page; the transference of a girl to a woman
contractually made by a father and a husband.

3.

Swans have no need for ink on a page to bind them
together. The male swan is called a cob, the female
a pen, and once they have found their one true
love they build a mound of sticks, leaves and moss
to prepare for parenthood. The Cygnus olor, more

commonly known as the mute swan, is not mute at all, driving predators away from the beloved nest with a triumphant call across the rippling water.

4.
Your own brood is small, a girl and a boy, four years apart. You feel the boredom of motherhood, the weight of responsibility equal to that of the love. When they are babies you write while they sleep, and when they are older you write when they're at nursery, and then at school. Your husband works long hours as a photographer, so you spend long hours alone or with the children. It is only with a pen in your hand that you're taken to a different place, the multitudinous words of your mind slowly unfurling to release the unknown things that lie dormant there.

5.
In 2012 in the city of Lakeland, Florida, two families brought two swans to live on the nearby lake, but the swans didn't know or like each other. They were kept in a pen to encourage intimacy, but once released the cob flew away, possibly as a statement to the family rather than his penitentiary cellmate. Finally he returned and they began dipping their bills to one another in courtship, but there is no record of a subsequent brood.

6.

When your children are old enough to hold a pen,
you fill their pencil cases with felt tips and glitter
pens, spreading the table with paper. They like to
make pictures of houses, and flowers, and animals,
and people with sticks for arms and legs. For
many years you keep your daughter's drawing of
silhouetted houses against a multicoloured sunset,
and in your bedside drawer is a Mother's Day card
that your son drew, seventy-three felt-tip love hearts
scattered across its cover. Around the time of these
makings your husband says: you saying you want to
be a writer is like me saying I want to be a rock star.
As you move through the house pretending these
words have not touched you, you feel the walls are
made of thick ice. You can see the world, but the
world cannot see you.

7.

A pen sounds to you like a gentle kind of
incarceration. The cage and the prison cells are
more brutal, a solid permanence to them that gives
liberty an unobtainable quality. But a pen suggests
a level of openness that means you could fly away
if you could only sprout wings, fly away to a shelter
with a stove, a table and chair, paper and pen – a
place of quiet and solitude. You spend many years
wondering how to sprout these wings.

8.

The green wings of Isis, the Egyptian Goddess of
Magic, symbolise power and mourning. When her
husband Osiris died, she fanned her wings to return
his breath. The ancient Egyptians liked wings on
their faces too, using kohl to frame and blacken
their eyes. They also invented the first pen, filling
tubes of marsh grass with ink to squeeze through a
sharpened nib.

9.

As a teenager your daughter draws thick black lines
around her eyes to match her dyed black hair. She
is old enough to buy her own cosmetics and she
buys other drawing implements too, pencils and
ink pens of varying thickness, sitting on her bed to
build pages of pictures. Your son collects notebooks
in which he draws and writes poetry. He is not
discerning in which pen he uses, but you often find
your own have disappeared.

10.

You buy new supplies of your favourite pen from
your favourite stationers, halfway up the cobbled
street in your hometown. In this shop you can also
buy artist's materials and gift stationery, such as
bicycle paper clips and journals whose covers are
embossed with green and gold peacocks or maps of
the world. For more serious stationeers, there is also
a multicoloured collection of Leuchtturms, your
own journal of choice.

11.
You have a new reason to buy stationery when you
begin teaching. You choose a medium-quality blue
ballpoint, a highlighter and whiteboard marker.
You keep them tucked into the cardboard folders
that you use for each class, and if you happen to be
in class without a pen you feel lost, even though you
rarely need to use it. Computers to you are fickle
things, but a pen is as reliable as gravity, as reliable
as the money you receive each month for your work.
You begin to feel the growth of small nubs on your
back, the gradual emergence of wings, perhaps.

12.
The squid has an entirely different form of
movement; a jet propulsion system that is protected
by a vestigial internal shell called a pen. This shell
is made of chitin and their tentacle suckers are
made up of suckerin proteins, which is similar to
spider silk. Both squid and spiders like to capture
their prey and, to avoid becoming the prey,
the squid releases mucus and ink. It is virtually
impossible to keep a squid in captivity as they value
their freedom and have been known to jump out of
tanks. They will also happily eat any pen-mate they
have been gifted.

13.
Your own tank becomes smaller and smaller,
the kitchen its centre of activity. Here you have
a ceramic pot that contains a collection of poor-
quality pens that are scratchy or blotchy or green-
inked. You use these pens for list-making, telephone
messages, and the ideas for stories that come to you
while you stir or chop or gaze from the window,
wishing for escape. It is here, while standing beside
this pot of pens, that you tell your husband you no
longer want to be married.

14.
The fountain pen was patented by the Italian,
Petrache Poenaru, in 1827, but it was prone to
drying and blotching. He died before the problem
was solved in 1884 by Lewis Edson Waterman, who
created three channels of ink instead of the bad-
tempered one. You wonder if Poenaru went to his
grave thrilled or disappointed that his design had
not been matched.

15.
Robert Adam developed his drawing skills in Italy,
during his Grand Tour in the 1750s. It is likely he
used a pencil and dipping pen, perhaps sketching
the Ponte Vecchio in Florence, an elegant bridge
over the Arno River that houses shops and cafés.
On his return to England, he used his pen to design
Pulteney Bridge in Bath, the place where you teach
now, the place that fills your soul.

16.

Whenever you walk through the Circus, the city's famous ring of townhouses, you look up to the stone acorns adorning the parapet. Your grandfather was a stonemason and carved one or more of these acorns, so you feel the fingerprints of your ancestry within the architecture of this city. He was given a book of architectural drawings by the man he was apprenticed to, a man named Mr Earp. Family legend has it that this man was a relative of the famous lawman, Wyatt Earp, but you have no way to verify this. Your grandfather passed this book down to your father, who also became a stonemason, and he passed it on to you. This book is so big and thick and heavy that you have to brace yourself when you lift it, and when you open its delicate pages, you find they are interweaved with tracing paper that bears the drawings of your grandfather, and possibly your father too.

17.

For three years Jane Austen lived a mere stone's throw from the Circus and the newly completed Pulteney Bridge, using a quill to write her novels. She knew how women were penned by the society in which they lived. Anne Elliot, her heroine in Persuasion says: Men have had every advantage of us in telling their own stories. Education has been theirs in so much higher a degree; the pen has been in their hands. I will not allow books to prove anything. Jane Austen never married, her writing all she needed to acknowledge the female predicament: a desire to exist beyond the stories of men.

18.
Some women have to become men in order to exist
beyond them. Mary Ann Evans used a nom de
plume and became George Eliot. Amantine Lucile
Aurore Dudevant became novelist George Sand;
and for a time, all three Brontë sisters wrote under
the names Ellis, Currer and Acton Bell. These
women, constrained by their gender, became free
with their pen.

19.
You change the course of your own story. You are the
swan that flies the pen, the squid that jumps the tank.
You continue to raise your children separately from
your husband, buying them pens and books and
plentiful art supplies for their drawing and painting. You
continue to teach, grateful that you have work that gives
you time to write, and to read the writing of others.

20.
In the 19th century pen factories of Birmingham,
the majority of workers were women. The city
became a hub for the pen trade, manufacturing
75% of the world's pen requirements. One factory
on Frederick Street is now a pen museum and
houses over 5000 examples of steel nibs, reeds,
quills and other pen paraphernalia. These pens
carried the touch of the women who made them out
to the towns and cities where they were sold, with
women buying them in increasing numbers. In the
19th century, more women were published than in
any preceding century.

21.

Your daughter is lucky enough to live in an age
when she can use a pen rather than build it,
although now she uses a plastic stylus on the glass
page of her iPad. Once a design is complete she
transfers it to a canvas of skin, the ink flowing
through her tattoo needle. She has sewn ink into
your own skin several times, flowers and branches
and birds, their flight a mere moment away.

22.

Your son has stayed with ballpoint or fibre-tipped
pens, writing poetry in journals or stream-of-
consciousness narratives onto rolls of paper like
Jack Kerouac. He writes on his paintings too, lines
of poetry or statements of observation – Mutant
thoughts of silhouetted angels – and you imagine
he would feel at home writing in the bygone age of
quill or fountain pen, relishing the labour required
for the smooth transference of ink to the page.

23.

You like to believe that if you'd worked in a 19th
century pen factory, you would have slipped a
steel-nibbed fountain pen into your pocket and
taken it home to a quiet room where there were
books on the shelves, books tucked beside pillows in
the armchair, books open on the desk beneath the
window. You would have sat at the desk and opened
the journal your wages paid for, you would have
uncapped your stolen fountain pen, and moved your
hand across the page to prove your own existence.

24.

You wonder if that woman is the same woman who lives now, writing with a blue Pilot G-2 07 onto a fresh page of her Leuchtturm journal. As she writes, the birds tattooed onto her arms stretch their wings, ruffling inky feathers in a shiver of delight before settling again to roost, unbound in their expansive state of being.

Always and forever, belief is everything. ∎

Writing

My Mother

by Sarah Young

Organs

Most of the stones on this English beach are pink. I choose one – brown-red and wet with creamy thick lines. It looks exactly like a human heart. Others are off-white with a tint of blue veins; old, bruised skin; marble flesh near death.

The stone only looks like a heart when it is wet. When it is dry, it is less fleshy. It does not glisten, it does not suggest life.

Alone with my body, I hear myself sniff. My feet are cold inside their large woollen socks. I am suddenly – aware of myself. Aware of how my body beats, moves, breathes; how it wrinkles, tightens, creates knots. I am aware of what else is patterned inside.

A rock pool barely rippled by wind sits calmly next to the rough incoming waves, separated only by a thin ridge of rock. I watch the waves further out, the way they lift and crest and fall, that familiar rhythm of tension and release. I think again of my mother, far across the sea in New Zealand. I spent four years trying to write a novel about her. I spent the last year trying to break the construction I created.

Four years earlier
The police were already gone by the time I arrived at my mother's house. She was sitting on a stool in the kitchen, trying to roll a cigarette with shaking hands. Her lip was swollen, the skin above it already purple-blue, a graze gently seeping blood, another on her temple. There was dirt on her forehead from where she'd fallen into the garden. Her pupils were wide and dark, her shaking head too big for her body, which was thinner than it should have been. Tobacco spilled from the trembling paper to the lino, this shaking at least consistent, familiar. The house was cold. The windows were open; they had been smoking inside. An uncooked chicken lay in a roasting pan on the kitchen bench, discarded hours ago for the beer bottles on the table.

A note on context
My mother left my father when I was two. She was close to catatonic. A few years later she enrolled at university, studied computer science, management and law, straight As but never enough for a degree. Some days she did not get out of bed. She parented me alone, occasionally enlisting my grandparents, before meeting my stepfather when I was eight. They married when I was ten. Fast-forward twenty-four years: I am living in London and she has gone back to him for about the fifteenth time. We have lost count. I have not yet lost hope, though my therapist tells me I probably should.

He has been charged with assault six times. He has never been imprisoned.

My novel – an attempt at articulating the collateral damage of this violence – was impossible to finish, demanding daily to be rewritten, to be written out again and again.

Story structure
An arc should not rejoin and complete itself. An arc should end, at least some way from its beginning.

———

My mother put down her half-rolled cigarette, tried to pour another glass of wine.

You don't need that, I said.

They've taken him, she snapped. What am I going to do? How am I going to pay the rent?

Mum –

No! I'm fucked. Her wild eyes looked straight through me.

We'll figure something out.

She shook her head, laughed grimly.

You need to go to the doctor, I said.

I need to pee.

She stood, wobbling slightly, cigarette seemingly forgotten.

I took her arm.

I wet my pants, she said.

What? Now?

No. Before. I still need to pee.

I guided her to the bathroom.

I didn't know how to speak to this woman. She was my mother – and she wasn't.

Formulating an absence

The novel fictionalised my memories of her, I
eroded them from my brain by placing them down
on paper; this seemed both a destructive act, and an
eminently sensible act of insurance. The night I am
recalling here is only one of many I included.

———

I untied the knotted shoestring that held up her
jeans, sickened by both the circumstance that
necessitated it and her weightless frame, then sat her
on the toilet. Her head nodded forward, eyes closing.

I untied the knotted shoestring that held up her jeans, sickened by both the circumstance that necessitated it and her weightless frame

Mum. Stay awake. You've probably got concussion.
She murmured something.
What?

Pee – on my – top.

She lifted her long shirt. I removed it.
What's that?
What.
That! On your stomach.
She looked down, momentarily confused, then
closed her eyes again and shook her head.
Mum!
What?
How?

He – kicked – me. OK?

When?

Last week maybe. I don't know.

Her voice was tired but angry; her eyes still closed, head nodding.

I'll get you some underwear. Wake up.

I ran to her bedroom, searched the drawers. I couldn't find a single pair of knickers without holes in them.

More promises: it'll be different this time, we're going to try counselling, yes lots of walks, no drinking at all

Two months earlier

I moved home from London after receiving a phone call from my mother. I was staying with my friend's mother, once the host of a home design television show, near Richmond Park. She had cooked my friend and I salmon steaks for dinner; we were eating them in her kitchen, which was full of nice things, celebrating something I can no longer remember. I apologised and ran upstairs to take the call.

My mother was drunk, crying; her words reeling. I made out: concussion clinic. Burwood Hospital.

I'm coming, I told her. I went back to the table, my hands shaking, and tried to smile and lightly converse.

Stasis

A series of moments all existing simultaneously.

For, with every message or phone call I received
saying there'd been an incident, there too existed
all the other parts of the cycle: the separation
and anger, the calm, the promises and busy
industriousness, the quietening, the sadness, the
depression, the drinking, the maniac recovery,
the days-long silence followed finally by news of
reconciliation, and more promises – it'll be different
this time, we're going to try counselling, yes lots of
walks, no drinking at all, I promise, yes a little fight,
who told you, your brother did he, he's lost his job
that's why, we can't pay the rent, the beer was on
special it wasn't a lot I just needed –

Silence.

And then - the phone call. The message. The
police, the ambulance. The shock to the gut.

This time – is it this time

Is she –

———

I flew back to New Zealand and stayed with her
and my two younger brothers in a flimsy statehouse
in one of the Christchurch suburbs worst-hit by the
magnitude 6.3 earthquake. The house was cold, the
city half-empty. She did not look good. She did not
sound – like herself. I remembered her words on the
call: *Strangled. Spinal fluid … dripping out my nose.*

She was paranoid, drinking constantly. I tried to
comfort her; I may as well have been speaking to

the wind. I ran out of patience for her sadness, her so-called love for him. We fought on my thirtieth birthday; she cried the morning after. Filled with guilt, I moved into a flat with friends near the red zone, an area of the city deemed no longer inhabitable where the land had sunk and shifted beyond redemption.

I ran daily alongside the river, winding through the abandoned houses, charting every minute change to their disrepair as they waited to be demolished.

Once upon a time

There was a bright line of light under her door; the clock beside the bed said 03:05. Her mother was vacuuming again. She was not allowed to get out of bed until 05:00. But her mother was. The vacuum stopped, the house vibrated with silence. She got up and tiptoed down the hallway, found her mother in the bathroom, scrubbing the sink in her long T-shirt, slim brown legs bare, yellow gloves up to her elbows.

Mum?

Her mother jumped. What are you doing up, monkey?

I can't sleep.

Get back in and I'll be there in a minute.

She climbed into bed and waited. Heard her mother walk down the hall, turn off the light. She came in and shut the door, closing them into darkness, and pulled up the chair beside the bed. Then she placed the egg, still cold from the fridge, on her cheek; began to roll it round and round, the shell soft and smooth on her warm skin. Her mother did this, for what seemed like hours, until she finally fell asleep.

—

A month after I moved out, my mother appeared to be recovering. We had the first big family Christmas in years – usually no one came if my stepfather was there. Everyone was half-drunk, and laughing in the pool by lunchtime, my mother beautiful in her straw hat, sunglasses and black and white swimsuit.

The clock beside the bed said 03:05. Her mother was vacuuming again. She was not allowed to get out of bed until 05:00. But her mother was

See, I said. Isn't this so much better?

My joy dampened at her stubborn silence, her half-hearted nod.

A week later she told me she was going back to him. I pleaded like a child but her face was unmoved.

—

My novel began in the red zone. Every day I added to the collection of images I was amassing of a city taken over by nature, a city I had grown up in and now barely recognised.

Security guards defended slumped and empty buildings, small foyers of light spilling into the black hole that the city centre had become by night. Houses stood empty, half-hidden by long grass. A bridge over the river resembled a helix: the energy and force of the quake captured in its new shape. Roads were endless detours, marred by slumping potholes; the aftershocks continued; the tremor moving my mother's hands and head did not stop. Suicide rates paused, then rocketed past the national average. The disarray, decay, dysfunction – became normal.

...held a packet of frozen potato chips periodically to my mother's lip, then to the lump on her forehead

I spoke to my mother less; it was the interregnum period, they would usually behave for a while. But less than a month after their reconciliation, my phone rang. This was the night of the melting chips, as I now refer to it.

———

The receptionist at the after-hours medical centre refused to look at my mother.

And does she … does she have a Community Services Card?

I don't know. I think so.

Is she able to … move?

She's here, isn't she?

So she had an … accident? Where is she … hurt? How – what, I mean…

My stepfather hit her.

Oh. Right. Well do you think she –

Why don't you ask her?

She didn't. We waited for the nurse instead. I held a packet of frozen potato chips periodically to my mother's lip, then to the lump on her forehead.

Half an hour passed. I took a photo of her on my phone. The blank look in her eyes changed, a brief flicker of lucidity and disgust.

I just wanted to show her when she was sober, to prove this had happened – again. That she had been lost, like she had fallen out of her eyes. I never did though – I didn't want to remind her of my betrayal.

Another evening, some years before
We sat outside the temporary safe house my mother was living in, drinking red wine. She told me then what my stepfather had done the last night they were together.

A squash racquet, hitting her head. A stepladder bashing her shins, leaving small fractures in its swinging wake. She traced gently with her finger the calcified knot of bone on her upper arm that she now needed an operation on, the place he seemed able to keep hitting with remarkable precision.

I listened to those words quietly pour out, to that careful itemisation punctured by moments where she murmured but I can't remember, not properly, where she put her head in her hands with a sigh; I always forget exactly what happened.

And all I could think was: you're drunk. You're drunk, again.

Later I washed the dishes, looking out the window at my mother in the dark courtyard. I tried to let what she'd told me sink in as the hot water scalded and tightened my skin; I tried to make myself see it, to force myself to hold those images, the racquet hitting her across the face again and again, tried not to let my eyes turn away, tried again to see this as something that really happened.

It wasn't that I thought she lied. I just couldn't believe him even capable of such things, could not believe that would happen in my mother's house, to my mother, mine.

—

By the time we saw the nurse, the bag of chips was nearly soft, a pool of water spreading across the cherry red linoleum seat.

Well now, she said with a kind but tired look. Why don't you tell me what happened?

The telling was for the police report. I told her my mother had been punched, multiple times, possibly strangled – I looked at my mother for confirmation but she only shrugged – then I tried to describe the older bruises I had found, one on her stomach.

The nurse frowned. Sorry. We are discussing this instance only. What happened this evening. That's all you need to tell me.

Goldilocks

My mother does not sit still. To be with her is to feel a mind and body that is preoccupied, always, with survival; to feel incapable of competing with the ghosts that insist on her attention, most of them still living.

But I understand this restlessness, this ceaseless disquiet.

My mother does not sit still. To be with her is to feel a mind and body that is preoccupied, always, with survival

In *The Art of Cruelty*, Maggie Nelson, discussing Freud, writes: 'The "compulsion to repeat" the trauma – be it in art, nightmare or waking life – is the organism's attempt to master the surplus anxiety that the original incursion produced'[1].

Surplus implies there is a non-surplus, an allowed or necessary amount, a certain level of anxiety required for living that is *just right*. How to know? Where is the line between enough and that nth tiniest amount too much? In many ways this anxiety feels unmeasurable, endlessly regenerating. Like a semi-dormant ember, it can light up with the barest of wind.

My grandmother says – *she's … OK I suppose. But she's still drinking too much.*

My brother says – *they're not great, no.*

———

1 Nelson, Maggie. *The Art of Cruelty*. WM Norton (2012), p11

The nurse was overworked and overweight, her blonde bob full of darkness at its roots. She wore silver bobbly ankle socks covered in stars beneath her blue trousers, dirty white sneakers. She wiped her brow repeatedly. She could not type. Her fingers kept hitting every key other than the one they were supposed to, they kept spilling over the side, trying to write something else.

Maslow's Hierarchy, my mother snapped. Go look that up. I'm sure he's heard of it, I whispered, feeling my face redden

Why didn't you tell me! She exclaimed, mostly at me. My mother was after all just quietly swaying in her seat like a drunk child trying to act sober.

What?

Why didn't you say it was all in capitals?

I looked at the screen.

I'm … sorry?

Hang on. We're going to have to do this again.

She stabbed the CapsLock key carefully then deleted the entire testimony.

Right. Let's try again, shall we?

Her smile still so doggedly friendly.

My mother too smiled at me politely, the smile that said – shit. I've just realised where we are. Oh dear. Let me talk my way out of this. Her memory already adapting, already changing. Who knew how the retelling compared. I still don't understand why the nurse just didn't copy the first one. And then – she did it again.

Delete.

Alright! That ever-cheerful nurse said. Third time lucky!

With unspoken agreement, we shortened the story to make things less painful for all of us. It was nearly 2am, the chip packet a deflated mound of wet plastic at my feet.

Then I thought we'd go home, like usual. When the doctor said they were going to transfer her to A&E – when he started talking about monitoring her, about head injuries rather than intoxication, cumulative effects – it was then that I became afraid.

We spent the next few hours waiting in a cubicle in A&E, my mother on a hospital trolley hooked up to a drip. The social worker interviewed us, moving clumsily through his questions. Has this happened before? How many times? Have you thought about leaving –

Maslow's Hierarchy, my mother snapped. Go look that up.

I'm sure he's heard of it, I whispered, feeling my face redden in my hands.

I went home at 4am, returned a few hours later to take her home. When we got in the car, she told me to go to the police station and pick him up. I was too tired to fight.

Earthquake
About a week later, I was trying to sleep when suddenly my body became not my own. I was divided in two; my mind was pouring out of my

skull, I was going to be institutionalised, I would never be the same.

The counsellor my GP referred me to smiled. You're not schizophrenic, she reassured me. That was just a panic attack.

I knew it was linked to that night, something about the blood, her incoherence, that bruise on her stomach, her skinniness. Something about the threat of permanent damage to the self, the fact it might already be too late.

My real mother had been wheeled out briefly from behind a curtain. She was no longer what she'd always been in my mind: strong, rebellious, unstoppable. She was becoming someone else.

Or maybe she had been for some time. The point was – I didn't know. And if this night and these injuries were real, then so too were all the others. I suspect the weight of that realisation arriving all at once, the years falling down atop me as I lay in bed, was what made me break.

The use of cartography to condense time
Imagine if we laid out the bruises on her skin – could see all of them at once, all the ones he made over the years atop and alongside each other – would there be any unbruised skin left? And could we draw the fractures atop that, veins of black Sharpie marker outlining where the bone came under pressure, where the bone failed, where the shock spread outward in cracks, fine lines?

What about the things you cannot see?

She has brain damage. She forgets simple words, says strange things; some days she cannot leave the house. She is also in her third year of an IT degree, top of the class, earning straight As.

This has been a slow erosion spread across many years. It is hard to map which parts of her brain have been altered, and which have not. There is no scientific measurement for this, no equation to combine the emotional with the physical, in order to read the degree of decline.

...in a land far, far away
She ran down the hall to her mother's room and pushed the door open, a wave of stale air hitting her. The curtains were shut. Her mother a lump in the bed, covers pulled up, only dark curls escaping. A pile of clothes on the floor. She ran towards the bed and then stopped. There was another body. A man with long red hair lifted his head, frowning, sleepy eyes confused.

She has brain damage. She forgets simple words, says strange things ... She is also in her third year of an IT degree, top of the class

She backed out slowly, turned and slammed the door, ran to the kitchen. Stared at the table, heart thumping, body shaking. Her mother's handbag lay beside an overflowing ashtray and dirty wineglasses, one imprinted with pink lips. She tipped the bag out, took her mother's sunglasses and held them for a moment, then snapped one of the arms off. Grabbed the lipstick slowly rolling towards the table edge, opened it and smeared it heavily across the wood. Broke the remaining cigarettes one by one into the bin, her breathing hard, and then slowing.

She ran out the door, towards the paddock at the back of the house, bare feet crunching on gravel, pushing her feet in harder, trying to hurt. She found her tree and started to climb.

When she returned to the house, the kitchen was quiet. The things on the table were still there. She stared at them for a moment, then wiped the lipstick away with her finger, grinding it into the wood. Got the Sellotape out of the drawer, sat down, and started trying to stick the sunglasses back together.

Another mirror

In Esme Weijun Wang's essay 'Diagnosis' from *The Collected Schizophrenias*, she writes : '... people speak of schizophrenics as though they were dead without being dead, gone in the eyes of those around them'[2].

While I knew my mother's point of view was not mine to describe, the act of writing her – the way she was gone without being gone, the pain of witnessing what I perceived to be her erosion – cemented her erasure regardless.

There is still something abstract about the woman I write about now, as if I consider only this meta-mother while my real mother exists on the other side of the world: reading, cooking, gardening, finishing university assignments, worming the cats. With each attempt to write her,

---

2 p3,4

she fades away a little more, and so I try to write her again, desperate to catch her, somehow.

Aftershock
A month later I was running through the red zone when suddenly I had to stop. It took me a few wheezing breaths, as if through a pinhole, to realise I was crying. No – I was sobbing uncontrollably, doubled-up in the middle of the road.

They were tears of rage.

I unfolded, waited for my chest to loosen, wiped my eyes and then ran home.

I returned to London a few months later.

Form and function
For the next two years I kept writing the novel: adding events as they occurred, changing structure and tone, trying to find the real mother, the real feeling, the real voice. At one point, I had more than 250,000 words. There was no arc, no end: only endless movement towards renewal.

I didn't even really know what the novel was trying to say or, more importantly – what it was trying to ask.

Shame
To be traumatised by another's trauma feels illegitimate. But, of course, I know it is not her trauma that wounds me. It is the loss of my mother again and again. It is the foreseeable renewal and repetition of this loss, and the knowledge it can only end one way – in definitive loss.

Perhaps this was why I could not finish my novel. If I kept writing it, she would remain alive.

Nelson goes on to say: '... these attempts [to master the anxiety] typically fail, often to catastrophic effect ... art can be seen as a relatively innocuous arena in which to showcase the failure – and to enjoy ... our symptoms'[3].

If then I am best to leave it unsaid, to deny this compulsion – where else does the story, the anxiety, go?

A further note on repetition
In London, I had a turbulent relationship with a French filmmaker who lived in Paris. Language barriers and distance provided too much fuel for my imagination; I feared his numerous exes, female producers, friends. He had an anger problem – childhood bullying and his father's early death anchoring a permanent feeling of injustice. He could not sleep without at least one bottle of wine, the dregs – often a full glass – skulled right before he brushed his teeth. My insecurities and constant questioning were fuel to his fire, the pretext for hours of shouting, glasses smashed, plates thrown to the floor.

He was not the first. There had been walls punched by my head, car dashboards cracked, glass doors shattered.

I wondered – with this man did I recreate the rhythm of my mother's relationships in order to understand it? By experiencing it, even at some lesser level, had I learned also to accept it? He and I ended our relationship on that very discussion.

---

3 p11

The skin beneath

It would take another year, and many more drafts, for me to give this novel up. Christmas was spent listening to my mother and stepfather scream drunkenly at each other over the phone. He had smashed her head into a wall a few days before. On New Year's Eve the police were called again, and my mother and stepfather split.

She and I spoke daily; my mother alternately drunk, sober; determined, heartbroken

She and I spoke daily, my mother alternately drunk, sober; determined, heartbroken. The benefit didn't cover her rent, she had no job, she was too old, she said, no one would hire her.

She became suicidal. I pleaded with my grandmother to stay with her.

A few weeks later, silence. I called and emailed my mother, fear ballooning inside.

A week later, she replied. They were back together.

Normally, I didn't allow myself to be upset; she would leave him, next time. This time I cried all the way to the tube station on my way to work. I was tired, I wanted this thing out of my life, this thing I could not control.

I realised – I was angry. I fired off emails telling her I felt betrayed that she had chosen him over us, that we hadn't had a mother for years; beating her with words, again and again, stunned and infuriated by her numb, cheerful replies, her refusal to respond to any of my points.

It had taken me so much to hurt her. To tell her: this is how I really feel.

Anti-climax
Some months after my outburst, I sent the novel out.

My mother and I inhabit different times and places even when we are in the same room, participating in the same conversation

I walked to work the next morning, suddenly alive to my surroundings. The black female teacher with the shaved head, pacing outside the gates of the Hasidic Jewish school in her bright sneakers in front of the tall, sombre Russian security guards, double-decker red buses hurtling past full of bright-eyed kids and bleary workers, huge autumn leaves falling onto the wide pavement, a man preaching about aliens on a megaphone outside Sainsbury's.

I felt something close to joy. It was not hopeful expectation for the novel – it was a lightness and relief that I no longer had to live inside it; that I could return to this world instead.

I received two rejections, five did not reply. I closed the novel file and did not open it again, without looking, I threw the piles of printed drafts – as tall as my desk – into three rubbish bags and hauled them to the bin.

Aftermath
Months later, I sat in a café in Iceland, eavesdropping on the couple next to me. My mother is stuck in 1989, the woman sitting next to me said

to her partner. Her cultural references, news, her life. I don't know how to bring her here.

Your mother is here, I thought. She is here – and there. Some people cannot draw the line between the two.

My mother and I inhabit different times and places even when we are in the same room, participating in the same conversation; fragments of her stuck in moments that I cannot reach: childhood abuse, rape, violence.

But maybe this is not even right. Perhaps in my search to understand her, it is my knife that cuts and scatters her across these timelines. Perhaps it is because I refuse to accept she cannot be happier, that she is not who I still want her to be.

Point of view
Nelson believes some works can still be worth persisting with for what they can show us about 'the sometimes simple, sometimes intricate ways in which humans imprison themselves and their others…', for how they can 'give clear pictures of these knots or binds, rather than […] hope[s] to offer a map out of them'[4].

I can say: this is what this feels like to be her daughter. I cannot tell you or her or myself how to get out of it. By admitting uncertainty and the ongoing prospect of change – including in our relationship – I will do less violence to her. I can create room for her – and myself – to breathe.

---

4 p11

Organ

The light on the beach is failing, the sky dark purple. My hands are now stiff, the tip of my nose numb. Gulls squawk above, the waves grow louder.

I look at my rock heart and I think: organs have borders. They know where they start and end, and where other organs and veins and things begin. They have a function, their own specific form; they do not inherit or mimic the form of another.

I will soon fly thousands of kilometres back to my real mother, the one who breathes and beats outside my mind. What will I find? What level of deterioration – or growth? Regardless of what this story may turn into, I have to try and see her as she is, without ideas of loss and negation and measurement, or even of what a mother should be.

I also have to try to see myself: my own story, a body and an arc that is not dependent upon hers.

The waves crash onto the sliver of sand before me. I watch them unyoke themselves from the ocean's larger rhythm, I watch them release themselves and their energy onto the sand and be swept up, yet again. I cradle the rock heart in my palm for a moment, and then I throw it hard, out into the sea.

I also know – I cannot stay too long. ⬛

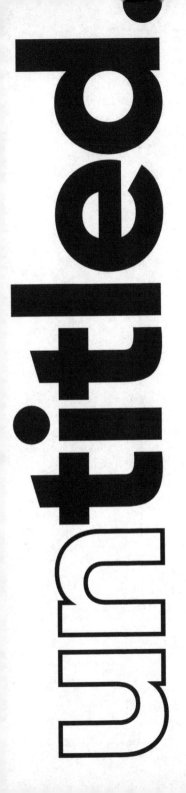

You thought you knew the whole story...

Founded in 2019, Untitled works to amplify and promote underrepresented writers work through regular Writers' Salon events, as well as *Untitled: Voices*, a global online journal. We welcome all forms of work in all styles.

Learn more about Untitled, read *Untitled: Voices*, and sign up for the latest news and opportunities.

untitledwriting.co.uk

🐦 writinguntitled 📷 untitled_writing

IN CONVERSATION WITH
Anna Jones

Anna Jones is a cook, writer, the voice of modern vegetarian cooking and the author of many bestselling books including A Modern Way to Eat, The Modern Cook's Year, *and most recently,* One. *Collectively, her books have been translated into five languages and have won the coveted Observer Food Monthly Best New Cookbook Award, The Guild of Food Writers Cookery Book Award, and have been nominated for the James Beard, Fortnum & Mason and André Simon awards. Hinterland editor Freya Dean sat down with Anna for a (virtual) chat to talk creative practice, inspirations, urgent agricultural issues — and of course, food.*

Freya Dean: I've wondered how the process differs when writing about food as opposed to other non-fiction subjects. Could you describe a little about your creative practice when you come to write a new book — what is typically the seed for a new project if you like, and how does it evolve from there?

Anna Jones: My creative process is quite fluid. The books are long projects so I will usually have a good bit of time to formulate an idea. It's really important to me that my books bring something which I feel is not already out there. That was easy with the first couple of books, as a lot of the writing about vegetarian food felt a bit fusty and brightly painted cafe if you can follow me. The more books I write, the more I see which recipes get cooked and which are useful to people. So, the sweet spot for my books is that they feel new and creative, using different flavours and techniques but that they still feel friendly enough that the recipes are cooked and become like old friends. I guess that is what gives me the parameters within which to be creative.

FD: Do the recipes come first, or do they follow from the stories behind them? And how do you bring all the recipes into the coherent whole that makes the book?

AJ: With ideas for books specifically, I tend to come up with a few different concepts — I'll have had ideas bubbling away in the background in my mind for a year or so — and then send a handful to my editor. We cherry-pick the most interesting bits from different ideas, discuss it all, and then I go away and have a rough idea of what the book will be about.

In terms of the recipes themselves, my inspiration comes from lots of different places – pre-2020 that was often through travel and meeting other amazing chefs – but more and more these days (and even pre-pandemic actually) my inspiration comes from boring things like trying to put dinner on the table in 30 minutes. Although I work in food, more often than not I still want dinner on the table quickly on a weeknight.

Seasonality is also a big thing for me. Obviously, the ingredients change throughout the year but also the cooking techniques, too. In the winter, I want to cook with my huge casserole dish, but in summer, it's a lot more about broths, light soups and salads.

FD: It feels as if each one of your books has a very clear thread running through it, but what's noticeable is that increasingly they have included another thread that's much more personal, that gives glimpses of your life – the recipes that grew out of your wedding breakfast for example, in *A Modern Cook's Year*, and the chard and ricotta pasta for your son. Was that a deliberate choice to move in that direction, or did that happen more naturally?

AJ: In my life, food and narrative are so intertwined that I think it's inevitable that I share some of the ideas, people and occasions behind my dishes. Maybe some of it is to do with having my own family now – I write about the food we all like to eat, rather than in my first book, which was much more about my own personal journey so far.

FD: On a similar note, to me the books achieve something that all the best non-fiction writing does: they are both very personal and of their time, but also universal and almost timeless – it's a really hard thing to pull off. Can you talk a little about that? Is it something you're aware of striving for, or does it emerge simply from the way you write and your approach to the writing?

AJ: Firstly, thank you. That has always been my aim with all of my books so it's really wonderful for it to be noticed. I want my books to feel modern and new and exciting, but I also felt that I wanted them to be books that I would be happy to pick up in 20 years time; to be able to cook from them, but also that I would feel proud of both the recipes and the design. It's been a hard balance to strike to make things feel fresh but also classic, and I hope perhaps timeless. My publishers 4th Estate and my editor Louise Haines are fantastic and they make such beautiful books. Louise allows me to be very involved in the design process — we invest a lot of time and energy in choosing designers and working with them to produce a book which feels both new and old. In terms of the words, I try to be relaxed and conversational without the words feeling too 'now' or using any language (or ingredients) which I feel will date. It is like trying to look into the future. I don't always get it right.

FD: Do you have a dedicated space for cooking for work? Is there that distinction for you? And where do you go to write?

AJ: This is something that has certainly changed over the years – my first book was developed almost solely in my own kitchen. Nowadays I am really lucky to have a studio, where I do lots of cooking for photoshoots, columns and books. But to be honest, much of my development and writing is still done in my house in Hackney.

FD: What or who are some of the biggest influences for you in terms of your own creative work?

AJ: One of my favourite writers has to be Nigel Slater. Nigel writes so warmly and with such ease and elegance that I feel as if I've sat at his kitchen counter a thousand times while he cooked. I could (and do) read his writing for hours. It's also so incredible that a whole world of online writers has opened up in recent years. Heidi Swanson of *101 Cookbooks* is one of the originals, and up there with the best of the best. Outside of that, the people around me inspire me – my brother and sister, my son, my husband, my friends – I think the perspectives of non cooks can be much more useful.

FD: And, perhaps intersecting with that last question, who are your favourite authors, food writers and otherwise? What are you reading (or listening to) currently?

AJ: This year I have been really enjoying newsletters. I write a weekly newsletter which shares many of the things that I read and listen to – and it's been amazing to see a real community form around it, especially in this past year. Ones I love to read myself are by Vittles, Mark Bittman and Alicia Kennedy. In terms of other food writers that I love reading — in no particular order — Sarit Packer and Itamar Srulovich of Honey and Co, Sarah Britton of My New Roots, Alison Roman, Laurie Colwin, Olia Hercules, Nik Sharma, Alice Waters and Samin Nosrat.

FD: The food industry is barely out of the headlines, with everything from Brexit to free school meals and agricultural practices. Is there anything that you feel doesn't get enough attention, that is still being overlooked and which people should be more concerned about?

AJ: Especially after writing *One*, I have come to realise there are a lot of things that need our attention more than ever — soil health is one them. It is absolutely essential. Soil is a combination of minerals, organic matter, air, water and 10-50,000 different living organisms. We need it to sustain life and yet we have taken it for granted; currently the world's arable soils are degrading at an alarming rate. We lose the equivalent of 30 football pitches of soil every minute to degradation and it is generally accepted that if nothing is done we only have 60 harvests left. The situation becomes even more urgent when you consider that it can take a thousand years for just one centimetre of topsoil to form. Put another way, if we do not radically change how we grow and produce food now, our children will not be able to feed themselves.

FD: And you yourself are clearly a strong public champion for sustainable food practices... I was thinking about how the big names in cooking and food writing have had celebrity status for some time now. How do you feel about that? I imagine in some ways it's helpful to have that platform and that voice, but also at times challenging?

AJ: I certainly don't see myself as a celebrity in any way at all. With success comes the odd time that I am recognised by people who cook from my books – which I love. But it's occasional and people are always so kind and generous if they do say hi. I have intentionally kept some pretty strict boundaries between my personal life and my cooking life. I don't feel comfortable sharing much about my family on social media (it feels ok to share a little more in my books). It's been a good decision for us as it's meant that my connection with people is around food, and that feels good. I don't want to grow my business to a point that some celebrity chefs have done, to me keeping things small and keeping a direct connection with everything I do is important. Not taking anything away from the chefs who have chosen to go bigger – I respect that, it's just not for me.

FD: You are very much at the vanguard of a new wave of food writers, and from reading the guest editions of your newsletter it seems as if you are now introducing readers to the next generation of food writers and makers – can you tell us some names to watch out for, and where we might find them already?

AJ: I feel very strongly that it's important to lift up the next generation of cooks and writers. When I first started cooking there were so few women writing about food; that has changed since, and in doing what I do I stand on the shoulders of the many women who did the work to allow this generation of female writers and cooks to come through. I feel it's my place to make sure that I now do my best to lift up the writers, cooks and chefs who might not otherwise have a voice, with a particular focus on marginalised groups and young, ethnic minority writers and cooks. Some current favourites are Alicia Kennedy, Claire Ratinon, Gurdeep Loyal, Nena Foster, Thalia Ho and Anna Sulan Massing.

FD: It's got to the point now where I can hardly remember a time when I didn't regularly cook either with what my children refer to as 'an Anna Jones cookbook' open on the counter, or referring to one of the recipes from memory, so I was first in line for your new book! Can you tell us a little about *One Pot, Pan, Planet* – it feels like a further distillation of your cooking and eating ethos?

AJ: That is so wonderful to hear, thank you. I wanted *One* to be both delicious and practical – putting plants at the centre of your table, and showing ways to maximise taste and minimise waste. I think we face such a complex set of challenges in today's world when it comes to sustainability and the climate emergency, that it's easy to be overwhelmed. I wanted *One* to offer incredibly delicious and simple plant-led recipes, alongside genuine, practical advice for how our small actions can make a collective difference. You can travel the world weekly from your kitchen with dishes such as Persian noodle soup, Korean car-rot and sesame pancakes, African peanut stew, baked dahl with tamarind-glazed sweet potato, and halloumi, mint, lemon and caramelised onion pie. I wanted to offer recipes for every occasion, from a weeknight tahini broccoli on toast, to puddings and entire feasts; and in the hope that these varied recipes become kitchen staples.

FD: And finally, given that book has just come out, is it too early to ask what you are turning your attention to next, is there a new project already taking shape?

AJ: I have already started thinking about my fifth book as I have an idea I am really excited about. That won't come out for at least another 18 months or so, but I'm excited to get going on it. I have also been working on an online course called The Vegetarian Kitchen with my friends at Create Academy. It's exciting as it the first time I have done something like this, and I have realised how much I love to teach and actually how much I love to use film to convey what I do.

For more information on Anna's books and current projects visit: annajones.co.uk and createacade-my.com/anna-jones **H**